To managers who see
their work as a calling.

ACKNOWLEDGMENTS

This book is based on a lifetime of experience, and it goes without saying that many people have contributed to the shaping and interpreting of this experience. I do, however, need to single out three colleagues in particular, for without their contribution this book would probably not have been written.

The first is Justin Ferrabee, with whom the seeds for this book were planted over a 20-year period. The planting process involved many animated discussions and whiteboard scribbles. The second is Brian Kelly. Brian and I have written several white papers together (available at Totem Hill's website, totemhill.com). Brian's assistance with capturing our discussions and editing the text has been invaluable. And finally there is Dr. Ken Suddaby. Ken is a practicing psychiatrist focusing on relationship dynamics. The genesis of Chapters 2 and 3, on emotional intelligence and relationship intelligence, involved many late-night discussions and brain-storming sessions. Ken did a yeoman's job capturing these discussions and producing the initial draft of those two chapters.

Thanks to you all – you have been good and supportive friends and fabulous colleagues. This book is a collaborative piece of work among the four of us.

PREFACE

As a young manager, I was asked to turn around a failing project. The manager I had replaced was a seasoned project manager with significantly more experience than I had. When I investigated the project, I found that he had done a thorough job on all things project management. He had put in place an excellent governance system. He had all the required work breakdown structures, PERT charts and Gantt charts. He regularly met with his team. He was on top of things and he held his people accountable. And yet, the project was failing. It certainly wasn't failing because of a lack of management – there was management in spades. Perplexing, yes?

The first question I asked myself was, "What have I gotten myself into?" If a veteran manager could not succeed, how was I, the young pup in the organization, going to fare any better? I should have looked before I leaped but I didn't, and now I had no way out. My first conclusion was that I was not going to out-project-manage my predecessor. My second conclusion was that everything my predecessor had put in place was necessary but that something was missing. My third conclusion was that I didn't have a frigging clue as to what was missing.

What I did know was that to do more of the same would only drive the project deeper into the weeds. So, I steeled my courage and I started to experiment. The good news was that the experiments worked and the project went on to success. The bad news was that my organization rewarded me. You guessed it – they rewarded me by giving me larger, dirtier projects to turn around. And so the experimentation continued.

Between projects, I would reflect on what happened. I would reflect on what worked, what didn't and why. With time, a repeatable approach for taking projects of all sizes from failure to best-in-class emerged.

The project teams I was responsible for were made up of highly skilled, highly educated professionals. In essence, I was leading teams of knowledge workers. These teams were precursors to the knowledge organizations that were to come. In the early 1990s, I had a blinding flash of the obvious: I realized that the approach I was using to drive projects up the productivity curve could also be used to drive whole organizations up their own productivity curves. The experimentation continued again, but this time the focus was on moving organizations towards best-of-breed status.

This book has one purpose: To share a model for building very high performance organizations, organizations that leap tall buildings in a single bound. This is a model that has emerged from 35 years of experimentation and learning.

Ron Wiens

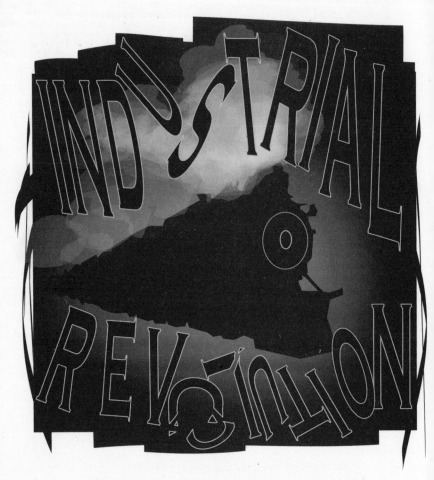

One example that we are all familiar with is the Industrial Revolution. Here the breakthrough was the steam engine.

CHAPTER ONE

INTRODUCTION

THE LEADER'S GUIDE TO CORPORATE CULTURE AS A COMPETITIVE ADVANTAGE

EVERY ONCE IN A WHILE the human race has a technical breakthrough that provides us with an exponential enhancement in capability. One example that we are all familiar with is the Industrial Revolution. Here the breakthrough was the steam engine, which led to the mechanization of work. Associated with a significant capability breakthrough is a radical change in what provides competitive advantage to organizations.

In the case of the Industrial Revolution, initially it was the machine itself that provided competitive advantage. If you didn't have one you couldn't compete and you were out of business. But soon businesses found that they were in competition with other businesses that also had machines. So managers worked to make their machines more efficient. Yes, they built better machines but they also did something else. They surrounded their machines with process. For the first time in history, across a wide array of organizations, structured, ordered processes (i.e., standardized work activities) were introduced. The purpose of these processes was to allow the uneducated farm workers who were pouring off the fields into the factories not only to work the machines but to work them so as to maximize their output.

So with the Industrial Revolution, we had the machine at the center of what was important to an organization. Good managers then surrounded their machines with good processes to maximize their return and then brought in the uneducated masses to work the processes. The machine was king, process existed to serve the machines and people existed to work the process. Outside all of this was management. Only management had a big-picture understanding of what was happening. Managers were the only ones with the prerequisite knowledge and education

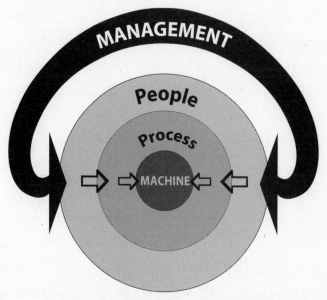

The machine was king, process existed to serve the machines and people existed to work the process. Outside all of this was management.

for this understanding. It was management's will that drove everything. It was management's will that drove people to work the processes that served the machines.

In the time since the start of the Industrial Revolution not a whole lot has changed in the way that organizations are managed. But something has changed. The human race is once again experiencing a technical breakthrough that is providing us with an exponential increase in capability.

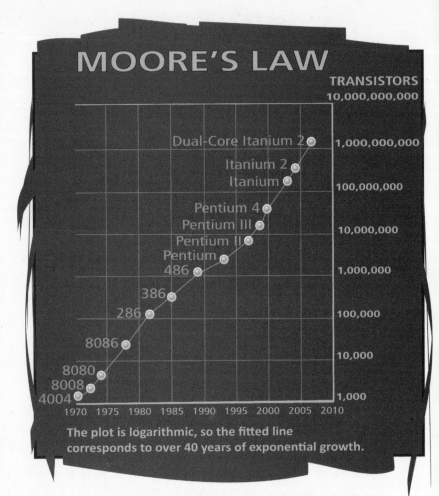

MOORE'S LAW

TRANSISTORS

The plot is logarithmic, so the fitted line corresponds to over 40 years of exponential growth.

Moore observed that the number of transistors per integrated circuit was doubling every 18 months. He then predicted that this trend would continue for another 10 years. This prediction has come to be known as Moore's Law, and what an incredibly wild prediction it must have seemed at the time.

To understand this breakthrough you need to go back to 1965 to the work of Gordon Moore, who was a young engineer working at an obscure little firm called Intel. Moore observed that the number of transistors per integrated circuit was doubling every 18 months. He then predicted that this trend would continue for another 10 years. This prediction has come to be known as Moore's Law and what an incredibly wild prediction it must have seemed at the time. A doubling of capacity every 18 months represents exponential growth. To predict that exponential growth would continue for another 10 years can only be called incredible. Well, what is even more incredible is that this exponential growth has continued now for close to 40 years and shows no signs of abating.

So the obvious question is, "So what?" Moore's Law may be of technical interest. Some of the nerdy group may even get downright excited by it, but so what? What is its relevance to business? Does it have any relevance to how we shape and run our organizations? Well, hold on to your hats, for this simple little techie law on circuit board capability has just reshaped what constitutes competitive advantage and as a result it is reshaping how we manage our organizations.

Moore's Law is taking us to an electronically connected world.

Moore's Law has provided the raw processing and storage capacity that has enabled the World Wide Web. Moore's Law is taking us to an electronically connected world. In the world that is emerging, people are connected not only to each other but also to each other's knowledge. The impact of this connection can be best summed up by the following observation made by Dr. Nick Bontis from McMaster University:

"In the 1930s, the cumulative codified (i.e., written down) knowledge base of the world doubled every 30 years.... In the 1970s, the cumulative codified knowledge base of the world doubled every 7 years." Bontis's prediction in 2000 was that by 2010 the cumulative codified knowledge base of the world would double every 11 hours.[1]

We may or may not have reached this 11 hour figure but what we do know for certain is that we now live and work in a world in which knowledge is growing exponentially. But knowledge equals opportunity. So this means that we now work in a world in which the opportunities available to us and our organizations are growing exponentially. And because everyone

---

[1] Dr. Nick Bontis, Closing keynote presentation, KM World (McMaster University, Hamilton, Ontario, 2000).

"In the 1930s, the cumulative codified knowledge base of the world doubled every 30 years.

In the 1970s, the cumulative codified knowledge base of the world doubled every 7 years.

By the year 2010, the cumulative codified knowledge base of the world will double every 11 hours!"

{ Dr. Nick Bontis }

is connected to this knowledge everyone is connected to the opportunities. So if your company is not pursuing the opportunities and the competitive advantage that is contained in this exponentially growing knowledge base, you can rest assured that somewhere in the world one of your competitors is. Competitive advantage today lies in an organization's ability to exploit this explosion of knowledge and see the opportunities before anyone else does. Those companies that can consistently do this faster than their competition will thrive and prosper while the competition withers on the vine.

There are several interesting by-products of this knowledge explosion. The first one is that the days of the all-knowing, all-seeing manager are over. It is now the norm for knowledge workers to be more aware of the new opportunities, on their piece of the coal face, than those who are managing them. Managers have not gotten dumber. It's just that there is so much new knowledge being created on a daily basis that managers can no longer keep up. If they can't keep up with the emerging knowledge and the opportunities embedded therein, then one of two things must occur. Either they burn out as they attempt to digest the knowledge required for quality decision-making or they slow down the organization in order to digest what they need to know. Either way the competition wins.

But hold on; aren't all companies in the same boat? If managers in one company can't keep up then wouldn't that be the case in other companies as well? The answer is yes. So who exactly is winning here? The answer is those businesses that are able to move decision-making downwards within their organization.

We said that managers have not gotten dumber. No, but employees have gotten smarter or at least better educated. Our organizations are now filled with highly educated knowledge workers. That is a key difference between now and 200 years ago, when our current management systems where invented. Now isn't that nice: We have an explosion of knowledge and at the same time we have growth in the capability of an organization's employees to understand and make use

Work was broken up into a series of small pieces or tasks.
The beauty of this approach was that an organization could make
use of large numbers of poorly educated workers.

of that knowledge. The winning organizations are those that have woken up to this fact. So what does waking up to the fact mean? It means a fundamental change in how organizations are managed.

Our approach to management, by and large, was created when organizations came, en masse, onto the scene – 200 years ago at the start of the Industrial Revolution. Managers knew everything and those who worked for them knew nothing, or at least very little. As well, as previously pointed out, the machine was king. The mechanistic approach became the model around which management practices were molded. What did this mean? Well, it meant that work was broken up into a series of small pieces or tasks. The beauty of this approach was that an organization could make use of large numbers of poorly educated workers. Because the pieces of work were small and clearly defined it was easy for the workers to get their heads around the task. All the workers had to do was focus on successfully delivering their piece of the puzzle. And if all of the pieces were successful then the whole would be successful. This is certainly a self-evident truth.

In fact, many managers today would probably make the case that this was and still is a fundamental law

The style is referred to as gofer management. In this style the manager is very careful not to pass on any big-picture knowledge to the employees. Work is assigned as a series of tasks, the results of which are assembled by the manager according to some greater design, of which only the manager is aware.

of something (i.e., the whole is equal to the sum of its parts). Anyway, under this fundamental law the manager's job became, first, breaking the work up into a number of logical bite-sized pieces and second, making sure that each worker successfully delivered his or her piece.

The Industrial Revolution was responsible for the creation of a management style that is still immensely popular today. The style is referred to as *gofer management*. In this style the manager is very careful not to pass on any big-picture knowledge to the employees. Work is assigned as a series of tasks, the results of which are assembled by the manager according to some greater design, of which only the manager is aware. This greatly reduces the need for employees to have to think on the job. Constant vigilance is required on the part of the manager; however, as Henry Ford so eloquently put it, "I pay my workers to bring their bodies to work and the bastards insist on bringing their minds."

This management style has served us well for 200 years. Well, it served the organization. Whether it served the workers is questionable. The style certainly did little to make work life an enriching experience.

Hold on, this is starting to sound like tree-hugger talk. The employees got paid for their work and had a much better life as result. If employees want enriching work then maybe they should join the clergy. I have a business to run. I am interested in what contributes to the bottom line, to my organization's success.

This is where it now gets really interesting. What drives bottom-line success has just gone through a quantum shift. The knowledge explosion has taken us into a new universe and the laws are different here.

How different? Well, the answer to this question takes us to the second interesting by-product of the knowledge explosion – the importance of organizational culture. (Several very successful manage-by-numbers management pioneers have just turned over in their graves!) Knowledge is everywhere. Ah, there is the rub. It used to be that if you saw a better way, then this insight, this knowledge, would probably have provided you with some sort of competitive advantage over a sustained period of time. Hence the expression "knowledge is power." If you had knowledge you didn't share it, you milked it for all it was worth. It might have taken you years to figure out how to deal successfully with your organization's suppliers and clients. This knowledge was reflected directly in your performance, it gave you a competitive advantage over your colleagues as well as over the competition. So sharing your knowledge was out of the question. Self-interest prevented you from doing so.

Well, something has changed and that something is the shelf-life of knowledge. It is near impossible today to hold onto knowledge and to keep its benefit for yourself. The knowledge explosion means that whatever insights you have gained today, the rest of the world will know next month. So the long-term value of knowledge has just taken a nosedive. Knowledge is still power, it's just that the longevity of that power has been dramatically reduced. Thus, today, true power comes from being able to constantly acquire and build new knowledge.

Wait for it – here is the quantum shift. One of the most effective ways of creating new knowledge is for two or more people to combine their existing knowledge to produce something entirely new. This is the basis of creative thinking. Mix existing pieces of knowledge over heated and excited discussion and there is no telling what will emerge.

So, the ability of people to work together, to openly share their knowledge, to leverage each other's insights, to create something new and wonderful on an ongoing basis is today's competitive advantage. How people work

One of the most effective ways of creating new knowledge is for two or more people to combine their existing knowledge to produce something entirely new. This is the basis of creative thinking. Mix existing pieces of knowledge over heated and excited discussion and there is no telling what will emerge.

together, how they interact, goes to the heart of what organizational culture is all about. Culture, a culture that facilitates this ongoing creation of new knowledge, a culture that is about people building and creating together, has become today's competitive advantage.

So what is the most important asset of the organization today? No, it's not people. Any company with money in their pockets can buy people. Enron went out and bought the best that money could buy and then promptly dumped them into a dysfunctional culture.[2] The most important asset of an organization today, the center of its universe, is a culture in which people are building and creating together. Building and creating together: nice phrase; what exactly does it mean? It means people sharing ideas, thoughts and knowledge with other people. It means people are listening intently to what their colleagues have to say, people are eager for their colleagues' opinions and insights. It means people being totally open with each other.

Now back when the machine was the center of the organization's universe, the role of management was to surround their machines with process and then to use their will to get people to work the process to serve the

---

2 Malcolm Gladwell, "The Talent Myth," *The New Yorker* (July 22, 2002).

machine. Today, management's job is to surround their people with an environment that gets them working and building together, an environment that allows people to leverage each other's creativity and knowledge.

This is starting to sound complex or at least circular. But it's not – complex, that is. There are three things that the manager needs to do and do well to build such an environment.

The first is to help their people to believe in themselves. Today's winning organizations are ones in which employees are taking themselves and their organizations to new places. They are trying new things. They are making mistakes, learning from these mistakes and moving on. When they get stuck or go off into the weeds the employees of these winning organizations are the first to recognize it and they freely put up their hand and ask for help. The degree to which people believe in themselves is a measure of the organization's **emotional intelligence (EI)**.

The second thing that the manager needs to do is to build an organization in which people care about each other. OK, now I am certain this is a tree-hugger's book. How can caring produce a culture that gives me a winning bottom line? The answer was most eloquently

Managers today are environment builders, not people pushers. This is leadership.

articulated by James A. Autry, the former CEO of the Crown Publishing Group, when he said, "I need to know that you care before I care to know what you know." Caring is the basis of trust. If I know that you care about me and my success, then I can trust you. If I can trust you, I can speak openly and frankly with you. If I can speak openly and frankly with you, we can solve problems together. If we can solve problems together, then we can leverage each other's creativity and knowledge to build competitive advantage. The ability of its people to trust is a measure of the organization's **relationship intelligence (RI)**.

The third environment-building thing that a manager has to do is to instill common cause. In winning organizations, employees have a deep and common understanding of the organization's desired future. But not only do they understand the organization's goals and objectives, they believe in them. Achieving them is meaningful. The strength of attachment of its people to its desired future is a measure of the organization's **corporate intelligence (CI)**.

Two hundred years ago, the all-knowing, all-seeing managers used their will to get their people to work the process to serve the machines. Today's managers build an environment that allows people to achieve the organization's objectives, not because someone is beating them on the head but because they want to. They not only understand the organization's goals, they believe in them. They believe in themselves and there is a deep-seated trust throughout the organization. Managers today are environment builders, not people pushers. This is leadership. This book is about how leaders use the combination of **EI, RI** and **CI** to build an environment that produces a winning culture.

CHAPTER TWO

EMOTIONAL INTELLIGENCE

EMOTIONS: SOMETHING THAT WON'T GO AWAY

I**T HAS BEEN THE NORM** across the decades in business culture to shy away from emotional content. "That is something that you leave at home." "We are here to get the work done." "Stiff upper lip, move on now!" Emotional discourse, especially with male-dominated leadership, is still seen as a sign of weakness. The truth is, however, that whether we like

> **Emotional intelligence is awareness of your emotions and the ability to use them to strengthen your performance.**

to admit it or not, emotions are rampant in all aspects of our lives, our society and our workplaces. Emotions are a fundamental element of human existence – as core

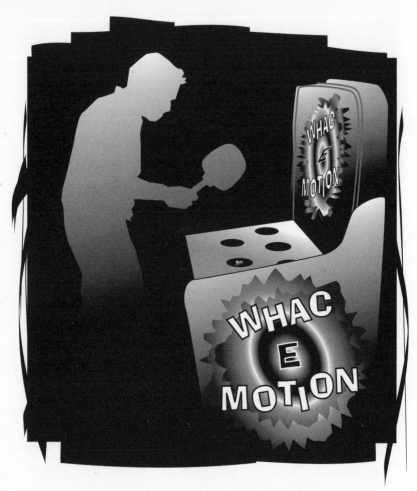

Emotional discourse, especially with male-dominated leadership, is still seen to be a sign of weakness. The truth is, however, that whether we like to admit it or not, emotions are rampant in all aspects of our lives, our society and our workplaces.

as thinking, breathing and beating hearts. Whether you talk about them or not, they are there. Whether you ignore them or suppress them, they are there.

So what? How are emotions relevant to solving problems, getting the work done, producing product? Well, think of it this way. Which person would you rather have on your team, someone who finds deep joy and meaning in their work, or someone who is in the wrong place and hates what they do? Would you rather have someone who is down on themselves or someone who believes in themselves and who is brimming with positive creative energy? Would you rather have someone who overcomes the bad days and maximizes the good, or an "unfeeling" individual who simply plods through the day-to-day work, never straying too far off course, but never producing much of anything new, useful or creative?

The answers to these questions are obvious. You want people who pour energy into their work in order to realize their fullest creative potential. You want people who are able to bring themselves fully to the task at hand. You want people whose emotions, rather than getting in the way, actually facilitate their ability to build and create with others.

You need people with emotional energy, not emotional baggage.

You want people devoted to their work and devoted to the organization. You want people who find and release joy in their work. You want people who fire on all cylinders, all day, and leave the office with more energy than they arrived with. You want sustainable best-of-breed creativity, from the senior manager who is deciding on the next product to bet the company on, to the frontline worker who finds a creative way to cut another 2 percent off production cost. You need people with emotional energy, not emotional baggage.

So now what? Does this mean that as a leader I have to explicitly work at building positive creative energy in the people I lead? Yes. Does it mean that emotions become part of our normal day-to-day business language? Yes. Does it mean that I have to examine my own emotions to make sure that I release my full creative energies and realize my maximum potential? YES.

Because of the globally competitive economy that we now work in, managers are required to maximize their people's performance. If emotions affect performance and if managers want to maximize performance, then managers need to understand emotional intelligence, and they will want to grow it. In winning organizations, every single manager needs to understand

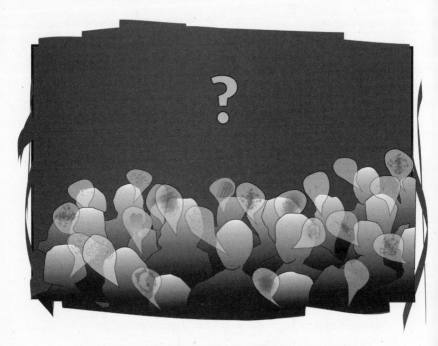

"What are emotions?" Ask this question of a hundred people and you'll get a hundred different answers.

emotional intelligence and how to make it grow to help their people realize their fullest potential. Fortunately, emotional intelligence is not genetic. It is not an innate skill that you possess or not. It is not something formed, by the age of six, and locked in for life. Emotional intelligence, like any other intelligence, can be grown in virtually anyone. In fact, it must be grown in everyone in the company if you want to have sustainable competitive advantage.

WHAT ARE EMOTIONS?

Ask this question of a hundred people and you'll get a hundred different answers. Our languages are rife with emotion-related words, expressions and sayings. You'll rarely read anything, short of a technical manual, that doesn't have some type of emotional reference. Emotion is deeply present in our relationships, our culture, our art, our music and our religions. Yet, we do not have a simple, society-wide shared model of emotional functioning. We do not have a society-wide shared language about how to manage negative emotions and how to build up positive ones to achieve our goals.

Scientific inquiry into our emotional lives has brought about a rich knowledge of what emotions

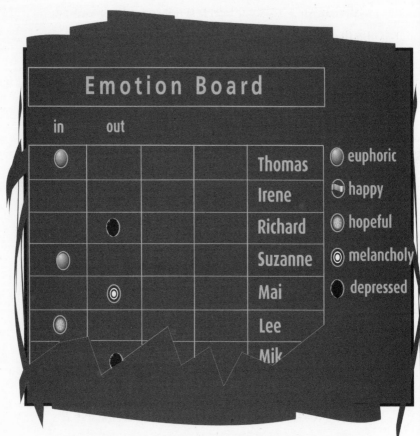

Managers need a simple, understandable, easily teachable model of what emotions are, how they affect us (good and bad) and how we can use them to reach our fullest potential.

are and what function they serve. From Freud, to Jung, to Oprah, we have been searching for some common understanding of how our emotions work. Unfortunately, this understanding has not yet been distilled into a simple common model that the masses understand, share and use. When it comes to a society-wide concrete understanding of what emotions are, we are still in the dark ages.

With emotional theory, we are at the same stage as before the invention of the printing press, when reading and writing were reserved for the elite few in universities or religious groups. Back then, knowledge was not for the masses. Today, a simple model of how emotions work is not available for the masses. It is kept for the gifted leader who uses emotional intelligence with ease, but would struggle communicating the method of their success to their students. It is for the highly trained therapist disseminating "expert" knowledge to the needy patient.

If emotions are to make a positive contribution to the organization's performance, then managers need a simple, understandable, easily teachable model of what emotions are, how they affect us (good and bad) and how we can use them to reach our fullest potential.

SO AGAIN, WHAT ARE EMOTIONS?

Simply put, emotions are memories. We humans are a product of evolution, and it is useful to try to understand emotions in that context. Most of what we have evolved as humans can be understood as a direct adaptation to the environment at hand – our competitive advantage to outlast other life forms. Essentially, emotions have evolved to serve two basic purposes: to protect and to (re)produce. Emotions of joy, attachment and pleasure have served to keep humans together, cooperating and, most importantly from an evolutionary perspective, reproducing. Deeply negative emotions of loss or abandonment have also served to keep us together – fear of separation or loneliness pushes us closer together.

But why develop these complex, ethereal, hard to understand experiences called emotions? Aren't they just confusing? Don't they just distract us from using rational thought to make the right choices? Do emotions really have any value? According to the theory of natural selection, emotions must have produced some evolutionary competitive advantage. They are with us for a reason. They are adaptive and must be inherently useful to us. To understand what purpose emotions serve for us, we must understand what they are. So again, what exactly are emotions?

Emotions are a special form of memory. In fact, emotions are a very efficient form of shorthand memory. When we experience something important – a graduation, the birth of a child or the loss of someone close – we will typically give a detailed blow-by-blow account of our recent experiences to those around us. It is natural to talk a lot about what we have just been through. This act of sharing helps us to emotionally process and work through what has just happened to us. Repetitively going over the important event through multiple conversations allows us to lay down long-term memories of the event, in the same way we memorize a telephone number by repeating it out loud several times.

But why go through this process? What is the evolutionary advantage to having memories? The answer is straightforward. The purpose of a memory is to allow us to learn from what we have experienced so that we can make better decisions in the future. Through learning, we constantly improve our decision-making strategies and this results in a higher likelihood of propagation of the species. Memories have made it possible for the human species to take over the planet.

Through rehashing a recent important event, we lay down detailed memories of the event. But as time goes on, the memory of the details of the event will naturally fade. We simply do not remember everything that has happened to us. Yet, everything that has happened to us has the potential to teach us about the future. This shapes how we make our decisions. But here's the dilemma: our memory of the details fades over time. Does this mean that our ability to adapt fades with the memories of our experiences? Not necessarily.

This is where emotions come in. Emotions are an incredibly powerful and useful tool. Emotions are a highly efficient way to distill and compact our memories. Emotions are the shorthand for more detailed memories of events. Simply put, emotions are strong shorthand memories. Emotions tend to fade much more slowly over time than detailed memories. Have you noticed that your memory of the *details* of an event fades over time, yet the *impact* of an important event can be felt in full force, years later, as if it were only yesterday? Remember when you gave that first kiss to your first child? Remember when your father, or your grandmother, died? The most powerful memory of the event is your emotional memory.

HOW DO EMOTIONS HELP US MAKE BETTER DECISIONS?

Through emotions, past important events can hold a powerful grip over us. Our emotions tell us what is significant and they influence how we act. Through our emotions, we are constantly provided with minute-to-minute information bytes from our past experiences. It's like a quarterback with a bug-in-the-ear receiving play-by-play instructions from the offensive coach. If we tune in to our emotions, we can receive incredibly useful messages from the past that inform us about what to do next.

If saber tooth tigers usually attack at nightfall in the forest, then it is very adaptive to start feeling a little anxious as the sun starts to go down. (Ever wonder where fear of the dark comes from?) Picture yourself as a Neanderthal. You have just stumbled onto a huge berry patch. You're very intent on bringing home as many as you can carry, and this is very likely to distract your conscious mind from worries about tigers, especially if you're hungry. However, your brain is also tracking the situation at a subconscious level. Your brain is working hard and fast behind the scenes to keep you alive and healthy. As the light dims, you start to feel uncomfortable and anxious. You look up and around a little, suspecting something. You then notice that the sun is low in the sky and you say to yourself, "Whoa, it's getting late. It's unsafe. I'll come back for the rest of these berries tomorrow." Your emotions warn you even though you're consciously paying attention to other senses like your eyes, nose and stomach.

So where did these warning emotions come from? Well, your tribe may have told you stories about tigers, or you may have been chased through the bush at dark one night, only to barely escape with your life. The memories of these instructive experiences were distilled into a compact, efficient warning tool for future situations – i.e., emotions. Without the emotions acting as a play-by-play bug-in-your-ear, you'd be walking through the bush constantly having to cue yourself: "Don't forget the tigers. Don't forget the tigers. Don't forget the tigers." You'd be so distracted by reciting this survival mantra that you'd walk right past the berries and starve to death anyway. So...you should listen to your emotions; they will tell you something useful.

However, these emotion/memory things can prove to be a double-edged sword. Suppose you're out picking berries and a dark cloud comes over. The sunlight dims as if it were dusk. You're likely to experience fear and have an impulse to go home (the tigers are coming!). If the fear is really strong, you may panic and run home, dumping your basket of berries on the ground. Ten minutes later, you arrive back at camp panting and out of breath. Then the cloud blows over, the sun comes out, and you realize that you've just irrationally wasted a good opportunity to gather food. (Not to mention the further frustration of seeing your mate with hands on hips and that *you-dropped-the-berries-again-you-idiot* look.)

What this example shows is that emotions can be very sensitive, but they are not necessarily very specific. In other words, emotions are designed to be easily, and indiscriminately, triggered. It is, from an evolutionary perspective, more advantageous to worry when you don't need to than to under-worry and ignore a deadly threat. Better to be safe than sorry.

This was of key value to our ancestors in their survival. Emotions were hardwired into their brains to trigger automatic self-protecting responses. You didn't have to think before you took defensive action. Your brain could subconsciously monitor the light conditions for you so that you could focus on picking berries.

Because emotions are not very specific, several

You may panic and run home, dumping your basket of berries on the ground. Ten minutes later, you arrive back at camp panting and out of breath. Then the cloud blows over, the sun comes out, and you realize that you've just irrationally wasted a good opportunity to gather food.

events can trigger the same strong emotion, even if the emotion isn't actually relevant to some of the events. A passing patch of cloud covering the noon-day sun is not the same thing as nightfall. The tigers are still sleeping.

So what is the adaptive thing to do with a strong emotion that could either be helpful or incredibly misleading? The adaptive thing to do is to be curious about the emotion, feel it, massage it, understand it, see what triggered it, and then, and only then, evaluate it. If you have the unfortunate tendency to ignore warning emotions, and it is nightfall, then you'll stay out too late picking food, only to be eaten yourself. If you tend to be over-sensitive to, or overwhelmed by, emotions, then you'll run away from your food source with every passing cloud. You'll starve to death.

The healthiest, most adaptive individual will feel fear at nightfall and go home. The same individual will be explicitly aware of fear during the daytime as a cloud passes over, deduce that the emotion is not relevant and then decide to stay on and continue picking. Which kind of person do you tend to be? 1) a berry picker to the death, 2) a starving runner or 3) a self-aware individual who has all of the same emotions as the previous two, but who is able to evaluate the relevance of each emotion

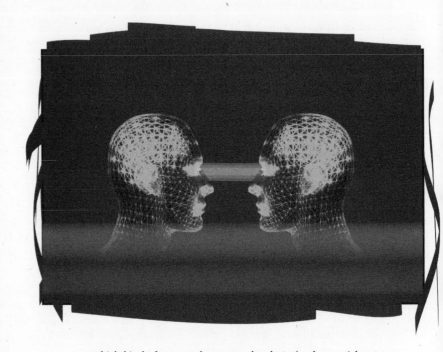

Which kind of person do you tend to be? 1) a berry picker to the death, 2) a starving runner or 3) a self-aware individual who has all of the same emotions as the previous two, but who is able to evaluate the relevance of each emotion, and then make the right choice, instead of impulsively reacting to your emotional hardwiring.

and then make the right choice, instead of impulsively reacting to your emotional hardwiring. If you are a highly successful leader, you probably answered number 3. Most of us are somewhat too far along the continuum towards either number 1 or number 2. The good news is that most anyone can consciously and explicitly move themselves towards number 3.

THE VALUE OF USING EMOTIONAL INTELLIGENCE AT WORK EVERY DAY

So, what is the value of using EI on a day-to-day basis? At a subconscious level, through our emotions, we rapidly process the collective wisdom of our life's experiences to inform our decisions about the future. Without emotions, this process would be slow, tedious and laborious. There would be no shorthand summary of our experiences. Instead, we would have to review all our major life events in detail to remind ourselves of the learning from each of them. Only then could we make a decision.

Imagine facing an important business decision and having to replay in your mind a videotape of everything you have done in your life *before* you make up your mind. Work would grind to a halt as everybody around the table closed their eyes and lapsed into a semi-comatose state of self-review.

However, unless we know specific tools and techniques, emotions can be tricky to use and interpret. When used appropriately, emotions can propel an individual to stellar performance. When ignored, or used unquestioningly, emotions can derail even the most talented individual in a matter of seconds.

Why is this? Well, it's because the very thing that makes emotions your ace in the hole also makes them your fatal flaw. Emotions are a highly condensed form of memory. They convey a great deal of important information in a very short period of time. The downside of this is that an emotion can often be giving you the wrong information for a given context. Remember, emotions are sensitive, but not specific. With our Neanderthal man, darkness appropriately triggers a fear of tigers, but to be safe rather than sorry, *any* kind of darkness, such as a cloud, can trigger fear.

A colleague of mine hired a new employee who was considered to be very talented. At the first team meeting, the new employee presented an excellent set of ideas to help the team target a potential new customer. However, her ideas fell on deaf ears because of the way she interacted with the team. She was aggressive. She was defensive. She picked a fight with anybody who offered even constructive criticism of her ideas.

As her first few weeks in the company unfolded, her aggressive style worsened. Nobody, including her, seemed to understand what was going on...until finally one day she had an insight. My colleague, the team leader, bore a physical resemblance to the new employee's ex-husband. Her emotions were appropriately feeding her all kinds of warning signals. Based on these warning signals, she defended herself from the perceived threat. Her emotions were desperately trying to help her. The only problem was, she ended up attacking a member of her own team who just happened to look like her ex-husband.

The new employee essentially dropped her berries and ran because a fluffy white cloud blocked out the sun. She lacked emotional self-awareness. She did not have the tools to be constantly aware of her emotions; she was controlled by emotional baggage. This little escapade took so much creative energy away from the team that the new client was lost.

If you are not consciously and explicitly aware of your emotions at all times, they can do you, and your organization, harm. A lack of EI can cut deeply into profit-making activities not only for you, but also for those around you.

EMOTIONS AND GOAL-DIRECTED BEHAVIOR

Leaders have always wanted their employees to realize their fullest potential. Leaders have always wanted their employees to give their all to the organization. In the past, leaders helped employees realize their potential through education and training. The assumption is that if you give the employee the knowledge they need in order to carry out a specific set of tasks, then they will be much more likely to get their work done efficiently and effectively.

In the past, this approach has worked. It is relatively easy to teach an individual a set of mechanical or intellectual skills, such as how to operate a machine, how to run a computer or how to organize a work team. These skills certainly help the organization to be profitable. However, things have changed and the set of skills that leaders must teach their employees has moved beyond just efficient task completion. Leaders must now teach emotional skills to their employees. Why is this?

The new economy is about constantly going to new places. In the old economy, the company would have a major new destination every decade. Now, profitable companies need to be able to set a new destination many times within a decade. This requires incredible amounts of change for all members of the company. This frequent changing of destinations means that employees have to be able to embrace change. If you lined up a hundred people in your organization, especially on the front lines, what percentage of them would be completely comfortable with change? Ten percent? Forty percent? Certainly not eighty or ninety percent. In fact, if you asked those hundred people what they think about regular significant change, you would probably discover a deep resistance to change, even if you are absolutely convinced that the change would be fundamentally good for each employee and the company as a whole. Why is that?

It is because change is fundamentally an emotional process. Goals are set intellectually, with the performance of the organization in mind. However, asking people to change what they do because it makes intellectual sense is simply not a good enough reason to get them to actually change. Why?

To a Neanderthal, anything new or unfamiliar was presumed dangerous until proven otherwise. Unfortunately, this still works for the majority of us today. If we do something really new, especially if it is really important to us, it will be, by definition, very uncomfortable. The Neanderthal part of your brain will be sending you warning emotions as if you were stupid enough to go berry picking in the dead of night.

You may have just decided, after deep rational thought, that it's perfectly safe to get 20 people to carry torches, scare the tigers and get a big stash of fresh berries before the bears get to them. This is a brilliant idea. You are working with the rest of the tribe to overcome the tiger obstacle. You've decided what is right and good to do, even though it's never been done before. But your *Neanderthal* brain doesn't care. It is going to feed you the mantra – night = tigers, night = tigers, night = tigers – until you try the new way a few times and you build up new feelings (shorthand memories) that tell you that nighttime *torch* berry picking is perfectly safe.

In short, the vast majority of us are doomed to coping with negative warning feelings every time we do something significantly new. This is because feelings are memories. Feelings are historical. Feelings are lag indicators, not lead indicators. It is very difficult to have only sustained good feelings about something that we've never done before. It is very difficult to *feel* safe with a situation until we have done it and we have experienced it to *be* safe.

New emotional memories cannot be created until we have finished experiencing the new events themselves. In other words, if we're going to use the modern rational parts of our brains to dream up new things, to realize our potential, to go where we haven't gone before, to *grow*, then we have to develop strategies to manage the negative emotions that our Neanderthal brains will inevitably feed us.

WHAT IS THE ANTIDOTE TO "CHANGE = FEAR"?

The way to overcome change resistance is to use a strong belief in self as a foundation from which to try new things and realize one's fullest potential. The road to realizing maximum potential is first a road inward. If I want to reach my highest level of achievement, I need to be explicitly aware of everything that I do well. I want to know what I am successful at. Not only that, I want to know what brings me joy, because I'm more likely to have staying power if I am working towards goals that give me pleasure along the way. If I can shamelessly shout out loud what I love and what I am good at... then I can USE it.

If you are sure of what you're good at, if you can trumpet your own successes, then you have set a foundation for belief in self. If you believe in yourself, then you believe in your abilities. But more importantly, if you believe in yourself, you believe in your potential to do things that you have never done before. You believe in your ability to take what you know, take your current skills, and then create something new…something valuable to yourself and the rest of the team. You are not afraid to stumble, because you know that you are a competent person. You are not afraid to make mistakes, because you know that you will learn from them and do even better as a result.

There's another part to the equation, though. All of us also have weaknesses – blind spots – things that we struggle with. We know that our evolutionary tendency is to self-protect. Our response is to hide our weaknesses from others, and even to hide our weaknesses from ourselves. Ostrich talk: "If we don't look at our weaknesses, if we don't name them, then they don't exist." If we avoid the substance of our weaknesses, then we don't have to feel *uncomfortable*. Who wants to feel uncomfortable anyway?

There is a cost to hiding, though. It becomes like a bad habit. The hiding becomes generalized and we often end up hiding our strengths as well. When we avoid intimate knowledge of our weaknesses, we actually undermine our ability to use our strengths to overcome them.

*Our response is to hide our weaknesses from others,
and even to hide our weaknesses from ourselves.
Ostrich talk: "If we don't look at our weaknesses,
if we don't name them, then they don't exist."*

Even worse, when we hide our weaknesses from ourselves and others, we forfeit the opportunity to ask for help.

When you think about it, it's sad. Here we are, bumping along, doing what we think is our best, but we can't explicitly say what we're good at. Society tells us not to. It's called boasting, arrogance, self-centeredness. Not only that, when we do get stuck, we don't even ask for help. As a leader, you end up seeing a bunch of guarded people who are unwilling to take any risk. How profitable is that?

On the other hand, the person who uses high emotional intelligence is willing to become intimately familiar with what they're not good at. They become intimately aware of their strengths. They first work at creating belief in themselves. They use their positive emotions as a firm foundation from which to look for their weaknesses. In fact they are willing to shamelessly shout out loud what they're bad at. They're willing to scream for help, without having any feelings of guilt, shame or failure.

The person who uses EI is energized by the possibility of realizing their full potential. Successful contribution becomes addictive…you want more of it. The person who uses EI won't let some dumb little personal weakness distract them from achieving their potential.

Areas of weakness are tremendously easy to fix. All you have to do is ask for help. You learn, through interaction with others, how to grow and overcome your weaknesses. You align yourself with others so that their skills complement yours, so that your blind spots are covered through team interaction.

So what is the antidote to "change = fear"? The antidote is belief in self, which comes from emotional intelligence. Emotional intelligence does not remove the fear of change. In fact, it teaches you to expect fear with change. It gives you the ability to make a conscious decision to effortlessly let the fear wash over you, and then you can carry on with the new. With emotional intelligence you are finally freed from your hardwiring. You will not be freed from being fed intense warning emotions, but you will be freed from the prehistoric hold that these emotions have had over you.

When the paralyzing impact of fear is removed from the change = fear equation, then you are able to look at the change for its inherent value and the opportunity that it will bring. At this stage, change becomes exciting. A new equation is written: "change = opportunity." As a leader, which equation do you want your people to operate by?

This is why, as a leader, it is no longer sufficient

When the paralyzing impact of fear is removed from the "change = fear" equation, then you are able to look at the change for its inherent value and the opportunity that it will bring.

to teach employees instrumental skills, such as mastering the latest technology. If you, as a leader, want to be profitable in the new economy, you have to help your people learn to believe in themselves. You have to model and teach a set of emotional skills that will allow people to get over their discomfort with newness. You have to model and teach a set of emotional skills that will allow people to realize their fullest potential because they are ready and willing to use their strengths and abilities to do things they have never done before. In this way, you have built a team that is able to take your organization to each new destination you set.

CHAPTER THREE

RELATIONSHIP INTELLIGENCE

WORKPLACE RELATIONSHIPS, A CASUALTY OF THE INDUSTRIAL REVOLUTION

PERHAPS THE GREATEST CASUALTY of the Industrial Revolution was the pivotal position relationships held in the work culture.

Before the Industrial Revolution, the goods that people needed were supplied by cottage industries – farming, spinning, weaving, making pottery and tools. All of these depended on families and the skills of several family members. The economic survival of these family industries depended on the ability to **create and sustain productive**

> Relationship intelligence is understanding the value of relationships, and having the ability to grow productive relationships whenever you need to.

Factories were built to house the machines and masses of people migrated from the countryside into the new, industrial cities.

relationships both within the family and with suppliers and customers. Cottage industries that flourished did so because family members (men, women and children) intimately cooperated to keep them going.

With the Industrial Revolution came machines that were built to do the work previously done by people at home. People were needed not to make the goods but to maintain the machines. Factories were built to house the machines and masses of people migrated from the countryside into the new, industrial cities.

Inconsistency and inefficiency had been the hall-mark of cottage industries that operated according to their own rules and were virtually uncontrolled by any-one outside. Machines and the creation of factories in which to house them meant that owners could herd their workers into one place, control their behavior and their output at work and generally improve the speed, quality, consistency and efficiency of their company's production.

Competitive advantage and profitability for a company operating from the late 18th century to the mid-20th century came from mechanizing operations and introducing efficient processes. The more efficiently a factory was able to operate its machines, the more goods were produced and the richer the factory owner became.

Factory owners paid a salary to their workers to keep their machines running and they created a hierarchy of supervisors to ensure the workers' compliance with the factory's processes. The managers and supervisors would be super-operators, more experienced in operating the machines than anyone else working in the factory. The worker's sole job was to implement the manager's orders.

The Industrial Revolution meant that the relationship skills central to the success of cottage-based businesses were no longer required. Investing in relationship-building between employees made no more money for factory owners and gave them no competitive advantage. Specialized skills were not a requirement for factory workers and labor was cheap, plentiful and replaceable. This was in stark contrast to the sophisticated mental and social skills and investment in people that was required in successful cottage industries. In the machine-based economy, only people's functioning bodies were required.

21ST CENTURY: WORKPLACE RELATIONSHIPS DRIVING COMPETITIVE ADVANTAGE

In our 21st century economy, competitive advantage for businesses has now shifted from serving machines, and training workers to be adept at running mechanical processes, to today's knowledge environment. The challenge for modern business is to create a culture in which these knowledge workers can be most productive. The rate of change in the last 50 years and the explosion of knowledge combined with globalization has made our economy complex. To get ahead and stay competitive, companies must:

- continually soak up new information,
- select information that has the potential to add to productivity,
- enable people to use new information to create new ideas,
- turn those ideas into products, and
- get those products to market faster than anyone else.

In today's economy, no single leader can be the central repository for expertise or creative thinking – there is simply too much information to take into account. Leaders who think they can perform such a variety of roles to the depth now required rob their companies of competitive advantage and are simply dooming their businesses to failure. So what does all this have to do with relationships, you may ask?

Well, the frontline knowledge workers are now the content experts. They are the most knowledgeable people when it comes to product and process. They are constantly scanning the environment looking for new ideas and new ways to get new products to market.

Each frontline knowledge worker is now doing what the industrial manager used to do a hundred years ago. Ownership of problems and initiatives for solving them have moved outwards and downwards in the company. This dissipation brings benefits in terms of enormous energy and creativity but it also brings problems. If you have a hundred frontline knowledge workers gathering information, what stops your company from spawning a hundred different ideas about where to take the business? How do those hundred pockets of information get shared and synthesized?

This is where the relationship becomes central – from the senior-most leaders to the frontline workers. That is because economic success comes out of not just the gathering of information, but the synthesis of information, the creation of new ideas and the alignment of those ideas for the achievement of a common organizational outcome. You need individual knowledge workers who are curious and creative to do this.

However, the power of synthesis and the power of creativity go up dramatically when you have two curious and creative individuals working together to come up with the next profitable idea.

> **Relationship intelligence is the ability to develop creative, problem-solving, profitable relationships throughout an organization.**

If I take all my information and all my ideas and put them on the table and you take all your information and all your ideas and put them on the same table, then we can mix them up and create a new, bigger, shared body of knowledge and ideas. Each of our knowledge bases gets enriched, and through discussion, we can recognize new patterns in the material. Together, we have a much higher likelihood of coming up with the next profitable idea.

In today's rapidly changing economy, the company that is able to get people building and creating together is the company that wins. The world has come full circle as relationship skills have again become necessary for economic success.

HIGH RI RELATIONSHIPS

So what do high RI relationships look like? What behaviors are actually observable in a high RI relationship? Typical manifestations are:

If I take all my information and all my ideas and put them on the table and you take all your ideas and put them on the same table, then we can mix them up and create a new, bigger, shared body of knowledge and ideas.

- People working together and producing richer solutions than they would have created on their own
- Open and honest communication
  » free sharing of ideas
  » confident sharing of incomplete ideas without fear of judgment
  » sharing solutions to challenging problems
  » people bouncing ideas off each other
- People enjoying each other's company
- Infectious positive energy and emotion as people view the results of their shared work with pride
- Knock-your-socks-off competitive advantage!

People in the high RI organization are not paid for cooking up good ideas in isolation, but for creating and maintaining a network of relationships out of which are born creative new ideas and effective problem-solving – all directed to the service of delivering on organizational goals and objectives.

THE CONSEQUENCES OF LOW RI AT WORK

In low RI companies, people do communicate, and here is what it typically looks like:

If you, as a leader, grow relationship intelligence in your organization before your competition, then you will be light-years ahead of them.

- People are sharing the bare minimum information required to complete the task at hand.

- Extra information is withheld.

- New ideas are not generated for the success of the whole organization but rather for the success of the individual.

- The reward system acknowledges individual effort and not team achievement of objectives.

- People do not challenge each other.

- Interaction takes place in an emotionally flat manner.

- Humor and enjoyment are little in evidence.

- There is sometimes open conflict.

In essence, the leadership is saddled with minimal productivity and minimal output. People might actually be accomplishing less than they would if they just worked on their own. There is no competitive advantage here!

If you, as a leader, grow relationship intelligence in your organization before your competition, then you will be light-years ahead of them.

THE BUILDING BLOCKS OF HIGH RI RELATIONSHIPS

So let's analyze high RI relationships. What is actually going on beneath the surface?

We know that the hallmarks of high RI relationships at work are creative idea production and effective problem-solving. So what makes a high RI work relationship tick? What are the building blocks that ensure creative ideas and effective problem-solving?

Actually, the answer to this question is surprisingly simple. The building blocks of a successful, productive work relationship are the same as those found in any successful relationship outside work. Think for a moment of any important, close, meaningful long-term relationship that you have outside of work – with a romantic partner, a family member, a close friend, a colleague in a community organization. Stop and think about what is common to all these relationships.

You are likely to have responded that you feel close to the other person, trust the other person, give support in times of trouble, are open and honest, have had a great deal of fun together and have shared deeply meaningful experiences.

You might have participated together in something

goal-oriented and fun, such as playing on a sports team. Perhaps you've raised children together. You may have focused with others on a project that has made the world a better place for others. In addition to all the above, think about the times you have felt most positively about yourself, with your abilities, your potential and your accomplishments. How often has accomplishing something meaningful been within the context of one of your close relationships – or if the accomplishment has been an individual achievement, how often has your first impulse been to run off and tell someone close to you?

You may well ask, "So what does this have to do with work? You're talking about my personal life, and I don't bring that to work.

Well, in our personal lives, we naturally gravitate towards safe, close, enjoyable, trusting and meaningful relationships. We tend to choose our friendships based on these characteristics and we put energy into those relationships. We work at keeping them active and alive over the years. Here it is: If everyone in your organization did the same thing with their work relationships as they did with their personal relationships, you would have a highly profitable business.

WHAT IS AN EFFECTIVE, PRODUCTIVE
WORKING RELATIONSHIP?

We have already established that competitive advantage comes from information sharing and profitable idea creation taking place within the context of effective working relationships. But what is an effective working relationship?

At all levels of the organization, if you and I are to work effectively and profitably together, then I have to share everything on my mind that is relevant to our success. This means:

+ sharing what I think will work and what I think won't work,

+ being explicit about what I know with confidence and what I don't know,

+ sharing half-baked ideas because you might have what's needed to do the other half of the baking,

+ being explicit about my knowledge gaps even if I might feel embarrassed about what I don't know,

+ challenging each other to get all of our ideas on the table – I have to challenge you when I think you are wrong,

+ boosting your confidence when your
  energy is flagging or you're distracted by
  other events, and

+ pushing you towards best because I care
  about your success and because I care
  about the success of the product of our
  relationship.

And now you might well say, "Hold on there! That is starting to sound like an intimate friendship! I already told you that I don't bring my personal life to work!"

Well, it all depends on how successful and profitable you want your organization to be. If, as a leader, you want a bunch of people coming together, working superficially, giving it their minimum and not really caring about results...well then, by all means, don't get your people meaningfully connected to each other.

However, if you want a collection of high performing, highly profitable relationships in your organization, then you need to help your people build the right kind of connections with each other. What elements do you think are required to make the high-performance relationships described above flourish in your workplace?

You're right. You need trust. You need

appreciation. You need attachment. Why? Because if I don't trust you, if I don't appreciate you, if I don't feel some connection and attachment to you, I'm simply not going to be *open* with you. Most people are only open with others once they have first developed a trusting attachment with them. Very few people will challenge, or allow themselves to be challenged towards best by, someone they don't know, respect and trust. The majority of us approach a new relationship with a somewhat defensive wait-and-see-what-happens stance until proven otherwise. In short, the relationship that I have with people in the work environment will not be highly effective or productive until attachment and trust somehow develop naturally. The problem is that in the workplace high RI relationships often don't develop naturally. The building of these highly productive relationships frequently requires some assistance.

BUILDING CONNECTION AND ATTACHMENT

This means taking a portion of every work day to learn something interesting about the people you work with. The easiest non-threatening, non-defensiveness-promoting way to do this is to inquire as to what people are passionate about and proud of, what brings them joy, and what they are successful at. This might be something that they have accomplished recently in their work in your organization, something accomplished in a previous organization or something personal – their baby has just crawled for the first time or their daughter's soccer team just won a tournament. They may have just run their first five miles or taken on a new role in a community organization. It may be the joy they just experienced reading a book or watching a movie, or that their favorite sports team just won a game.

In fact, if you encourage everyone in your organization to start every work interaction with an enquiry about something interesting and positive, then you are explicitly highlighting the importance of connection as a foundation for a successful work interaction.

"Fine!" you say. "Now you're back to telling me that I have to make friends with everyone at work again!"

Hmm…well, actually you are right. While you don't have to foster close personal relationships with everyone in the organization, you do need to promote friendly relationships between people at work – appropriately geared to the level of collaboration that

Building connection and attachment means taking a portion of every work day to learn something interesting about the people you work with.

is required between them. Even if the work contact is casual and infrequent, fostering open connections will sustain your organization well and will build a culture of appreciation, support, trust and openness – a winning culture.

To develop a connection and attachment with other people you need to develop an appreciation of them; to do this, you need to get to know them.

It usually takes a minimum of six months and often 12 to 18 months for high RI relationships to develop on their own. Your organization, if it's like most, is experiencing rapid and ongoing change. People are moving around within the organization and people are coming and going all the time. Can your profitability wait a year and a half every time a new team is formed? As a leader, you simply can't bet your business on the slow natural development of successful working relationships. You need to do something to make sure that they happen, now.

So how do you build a high RI organization? How do you, as a leader, foster and grow RI in your organization for competitive advantage? Well, you need a simple, understandable, learnable, repeatable, easily communicated model of how relationships work.

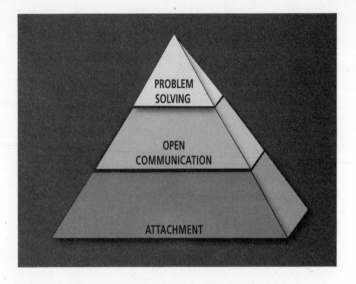

BUILDING SUCCESSFUL RELATIONSHIPS –
A THREE-LEVEL PYRAMID

There are three stages to the development of successful relationships:

1. Attachment

2. Open communication

3. Problem-solving

These three levels exist in all successful relationships. The first level must be in place before the others can be added.

ATTACHMENT is the foundation for the relationship. It is the connection that allows the development of trust.

OPEN COMMUNICATION is added when attachment and trust exist. If I trust you, then I am free to communicate openly and honestly with you. I can share everything that is on my mind.

PROBLEM-SOLVING becomes possible when the first two levels are in place. With the open sharing of information, we can now take our collaboration, problem-solving and creativity to new heights.

SUSTAINING PRODUCTIVE RELATIONSHIPS

Once a relationship is built, it has to be actively maintained. Every living thing, every person, every system, every organization and every relationship is constantly growing or declining.

When we successfully build a relationship, we use a set of understandings, assumptions and skills that are appropriate to the moment. Yet in a rapidly changing world, the set of assumptions on which we built the relationship will quickly become outdated. What I think I know about you and how we work best together are constantly changing. That means that I need to constantly adapt how I interact with you.

In the service of getting the work done, we often drift, we get used to each other and forget to communicate or share critical information. And once we've stopped pursuing lively, interactive and frank conversations with each other for a little while, we get used to their absence. Like stopping exercise for too long, it gets harder to get back to it, and it can really be uncomfortable when you do!

OBSERVATION TOWER: SYSTEM AWARENESS

Think of system awareness as sitting on top of the whole of the pyramid, like an eye keeping watch over the whole relationship. System awareness means constantly evaluating work relationships to see whether they are working effectively. You need to be ready to intervene to keep your relationships healthy and productive. As a leader, you need to be ready to intervene with others to help them build the system awareness necessary to keep their relationships healthy and productive.

You may think that sounds exhausting, and that it's hard enough just to try to meet all the business demands placed on you. It's not as challenging as it sounds. All it means is routinely paying attention to the three levels of the relationship pyramid:

1. Attachment
2. Open communication
3. Problem-solving

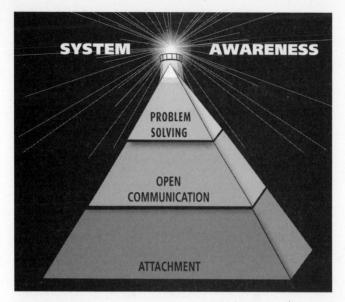

You need to:

+ Make sure that you are routinely
  working on attachment by asking co-
  workers questions about the things they
  are passionate about outside work. You
  might get together for lunch, just to share
  some food and conversation.

+ Support open communication by creating
  a habit of having a frank, open conversation with at least one person every day.

+ Support problem-solving by asking a
  coworker to participate in a brain-
  storming session.

System awareness is about keeping all your working relationships well oiled and tuned up.

Society has come full circle, from the family, relationship-based cottage industries, through the isolated and sterile work life of the Industrial Revolution factory worker, to the knowledge workers of the modern Information Age, who must develop proficiency in relationship skills to bring competitive advantage to their organization.

We are poised on the edge of a new age in which those organizations that help their people create healthy, vibrant, creative relationships are those organizations that will outperform their competitors. The organizational culture that fosters and nurtures relationships is a winning culture. Healthy, vibrant relationships have become the core of competitive advantage.

CHAPTER FOUR

CORPORATE INTELLIGENCE

SMART WORKERS WANTING TO DO GOOD

}**ORGANIZATIONS ARE FILLED** with well-educated, hard-working individuals who are motivated to "do good." People are working longer and harder than ever — so much so that a whole industry has built up around helping people manage the stress of their jobs. It is part of the human condition to want to make a difference. Most people want to be able to look back over their lives and say, "the world is at least a little better for my existence." For many, if not most, working with

> Corporate intelligence is about being able to deeply connect people with a common future so that the people of the organization are able to align and collectively pour their energy into achieving this future.

others in an organization is the vehicle through which they make their contribution.

So, the obvious questions that a leader should be asking are, "If my organization is filled with these insightful, well-educated, hard-working, motivated individuals, why isn't my organization *leaping tall buildings in a single bound?* Why is it so hard to move my organization forward? Why does this year feel so much like last year and the year before that?"

The answer is, lack of common cause. In the absence of common cause, people come to work just to earn money, or create their own cause and go off in all directions. As Charles Handy so succinctly put it,

> "If you want to retain talent, you've got to create cause. Otherwise you get a purely instrumental relationship in which I'm working for you purely because I'm earning money, or because it's teaching me some skills which I will go somewhere else and use. Then you get very short-term thinking, very selfish thinking."[3]

---

3 Charles Handy, "Finding Sense in Uncertainty." In Rowan Gibson (Ed.), *Rethinking the Future* (London: Nicholas Brealey, 1998).

COMMON CAUSE:
PREDICTOR OF PERFORMANCE AND SUCCESS

In all the organizations that we have worked with, from small to large, public and private, we have found the degree to which common cause exists to be one of the most insightful predictors of performance and success. Without common cause, there is no common understanding of the organization's desired future and its business goals. Without common cause, we are like the blind. We imagine that the part of the elephant that we are touching defines the beast.

Without common cause, individuals rely on implicit assumptions and beliefs to shape decisions about business needs and priorities. Yes, people are educated. Yes, they are working hard. And yes, they are motivated to "do good." But here is the rub: without common cause, your people all have their own personal definition of what doing good means.

THE LEADERS' JOB: BUILDING COMMON CAUSE

It is the leader's job to build a clear and common picture, across the organization, of the targeted future. Failure to do so creates a vacuum. But this vacuum does not stay empty very long. People fill it with their own definition of success. This leads people to focus on their own success or at best the success of their particular piece of the business rather than the success of the business as a whole. The result is an organization in which people are going down competing paths with all the inconsistent and counterproductive decisions that go along with this. Corporate planning becomes a process of competing agendas. Managers operate autonomously and not as a team. Because they do not share a common destination, people are not able to build on each other's success.

THE INCANDESCENT ORGANIZATION

Organizations without common cause are like the incandescent light bulb: lots of energy being expended, but it's all going in different directions. The result: tracking the organization's progress is a lot like watching molasses flow. In organizations with low corporate intelligence, individual efforts are not aligned; everyone is going off in different directions trying to make the organization successful. A great deal of energy is expended but little gets accomplished. This year ends up looking a whole lot like last year.

THE POWER SOURCE FOR ORGANIZATIONAL PERFORMANCE

Cause gives people courage. Cause gives people the reason to endure the pain of change. Common cause creates a company whose people are striding arm in arm towards the company's desired future. In essence, deeply held common cause leads to a company of zealots with the courage and energy needed to tackle the barriers and hurdles that block the pathway to the organization's desired future.

When an organization's people are deeply connected to a common cause they genuinely care about the success of the whole. This caring is the power source for organizational performance.

WORKING FOR THE GOOD OF THE WHOLE

We have observed that one of the characteristics of a high-performance organization is that the people

*Common cause creates a company whose people are striding
arm in arm towards the company's desired future.*

within it are willing to sub-optimize their piece of the business for the good of the whole. Now this statement sounds contradictory. How can deliberate sub-optimization of a piece of the business improve the performance of the whole?

To understand the connection between sub-optimization and increasing performance, consider the following case study.

A company had undertaken a major rewrite of one of its legacy information technology systems. This rewrite was absolutely critical to the organization's ability to compete in its market space. The project involved close to 100 people. It was expected that the project would take about three years to complete. Successful delivery of such a project is non-trivial to say the least. The global failure rate for large IT projects such as this is close to 70 percent.

The systems integrator contracted for the job was very experienced in this type of large IT systems delivery. They selected one of their most experienced managers to lead the project. He in turn assembled a team of seasoned professionals, many of whom he had successfully worked with before. Of particular relevance to this case study is the systems integrator's test team.

In essence, deeply held common cause leads to a company of zealots with the courage and energy needed to tackle the barriers and hurdles that block the pathway to the organization's desired future.

The test team was well staffed. They had a well-defined and proven methodology for testing systems. They rigorously tested the programs that came out of the development team. They did an excellent job of identifying problems and promptly alerting the development team as to the required rework. This test team did everything that a test team was supposed to do and they did it well.

However, the client became increasingly alarmed about the systems integrator's ability to deliver what was needed in the agreed upon timeframe. So alarmed in fact, that after 18 months the client decided to cut their losses and removed the systems integrator from the project. The client assessed what had been delivered and came to the conclusion that very little was salvageable. In essence, the client came to the conclusion that the project would have to be restarted essentially from the beginning. The client was left with no alternative than to bring in a new systems integration firm and relaunch the project.

The new firm had less rigorous practices and methodologies than the original contractor. Its test team was much smaller and less experienced than the previous one. The new test team did not arrive with a formal tried and true methodology. They had to develop one before

Clearly the first test team defined success not by the success of the whole, but rather by the success of their piece of the whole.

they could start their work. Compared to the previous test team, the new team was green to say the least. But this smaller green test team had one **major advantage.** They were part of a larger team that had common cause.

To assist with the project's relaunch, a project coach was brought in to assist the project's management team in building EI, RI and CI. As a result the project's management team worked relentlessly at connecting their people to cause. They helped their people understand why the project was worthy of their time. They helped their people understand the contribution that their work would be making to the client's well being (i.e., the ability of the client to compete in its selected market space).

What is interesting about the first test team is that when their project failed, the members of the test team were proud of their work and the work of their team. They did not feel that they wore any responsibility for the failure of the project. Clearly the first team defined success not by the success of the whole, but rather by the success of their piece of the whole.

The actions of the second test team showed that they had quite a different definition of success. When the second team started their testing on the first release of programs, they noticed right away that the programs had an unusually high number of errors. This they interpreted as poor quality control on the part of the programmers. The programmers were supposed to be unit testing their programs before handing them over to the test team. This would allow the test team to focus more on systems testing; that is, how a group of programs work together.

The test team, by identifying the problem and returning the problem programs to the programmers, had done their job and done it well. The second test team could have stopped here and taken pride in their performance. Certainly, this is what the first team did.

However, the second team further surmised, quite correctly, that unless the programmers improved the quality of their programming, the amount of retesting required would adversely affect the project schedule. So without asking permission, and remember that the second test team was thinly staffed in comparison to the first team, two members of the test team relocated their desks to the programmers' section.

These two test team members then worked directly with the programmers, helping them develop a quality control process for their programs. The outcome was that the quality of the programs rose sharply. Clearly, the second test team, the green team, as a result of the cultural work done by their managers, came to see the success of the test team as secondary to the success of the project as a whole. Thus, the green team was willing to sub-optimize their piece of the project, giving up two resources when they could ill afford to do so, because this was what was needed for project success.

In the end, the project was a phenomenal success, finishing ahead of schedule and beating the industry average for quality (as measured by the number of errors found in the first three months of production) by a factor of 10 and coming in at one-third of the industry average cost for a system of its size.

THE LASER ORGANIZATION

Low CI organizations – those without common cause – are incandescent in that individual efforts are not aligned; everyone is going off in different directions. High CI organizations are laser-like because they consist of people who are traveling in the same direction. These are people who share a common

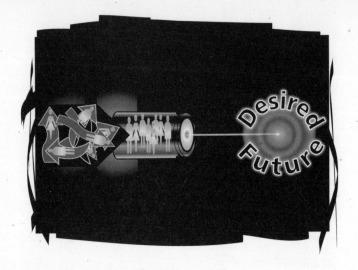

understanding of their organization's desired future and believe that the achievement of this future is worthy of their time.

Lasers are all about the alignment (the phase synchronization) of light. A high CI organization synchronizes the organization's energy around common goals. At the highest level, a laser organization is self-sustaining because its members are constantly reconnecting each other with the organization's goals and as a result constantly re-energizing each other towards the attainment of these goals. The result is an organization that is able to do more and go further while providing its people with a rich work experience.

THE FIVE LEVELS OF CORPORATE INTELLIGENCE

The figure below shows the five levels of corporate intelligence, with a level 1 organization having the least and a level 5 having the most CI.

LEVEL 1. In our experience, 80 percent or more of organizations are at level 1. These organizations are highly incandescent. Ask any 10 members in a level 1 organization what their company's goals are and you most likely will get 10 different answers, if you get any answers at all.

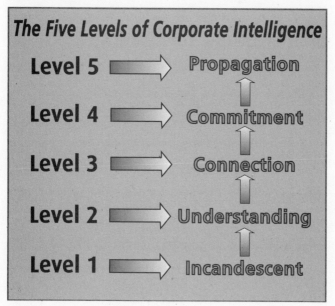

LEVEL 2. If an organization has been able to build common understanding – across the majority of its people, of its desired future and the goals that have been set to get it there – then this organization will have achieved level 2 CI status. This means that by simply building common understanding among its people of the desired future, an organization will be in the top 20 percent of organizations in terms of CI development.

Level 2 organizations get everyone onto the same page. Everyone has the same understanding of where the organization is heading.

LEVEL 3. To achieve level 3 CI status, an organization must not only build understanding of the desired future but also belief, among its people, that putting energy into the attainment of this future is worthy of one's time.

A level 3 organization not only gets its people aligned around its goals but it gets them wanting to achieve them. An organization that has achieved level 3 status has connected its people to the desired future.

Now, here is the paradox. An organization can achieve level 3 CI status and still not have its people energetically working towards the achievement of the desired future. How can this be? You have people who both understand and believe in

ANNUAL DRAGON BOAT RACES
CELEBRATE OUR VOLUNTEERS

To achieve level 3 CI status, an organization must not only build understanding of the desired future but also belief, among its people, that putting energy into the attainment of this future is worthy of one's time.

their organization's desired future and yet they are not putting body and soul into its realization. The answer to this paradox is that while the people believe in the organization's desired future, they do not have faith in the courage of their managers to maintain the course when the going gets tough.

Organizations get stuck at level 3 because their people have experienced being energized, taking personal initiatives to pursue the organization's goals and then being abandoned by their managers when things have not worked out as planned.

LEVEL 4. To achieve level 4 status, managers need to find ways to demonstrate to their people that they are serious about achieving their organization's desired future. People need to:

+ believe that their managers have the courage to do what it takes to make the organization successful,
+ see their managers taking real risk, intelligently, in the achievement of the organization's desired future, and
+ see their managers standing behind them when they take a reasonable risk and things do not go as planned.

There are no shortcuts to achieving level 4 status. It takes time. Achieving level 4 status is all about managers building their personal credibility with their people. The moment this credibility is compromised, the organization's corporate intelligence will be eroded. Organizations that have reached level 4 CI status are made up of people who:

- understand the organization's desired future,
- believe that the achievement of it is worthy of their time, and
- are committed to making it happen.

Level 4 organizations have not only engaged their people's heads and hearts, they have also been successful in getting their people's feet in motion.

Very few organizations make it to level 4. Although getting to level 4 is not complicated, it's not easy. Getting to level 4 requires every manager at every level in the organization to be talking regularly about the organization's future, its goals and its objectives. Managers have to be constantly painting a picture of where the organization is going.

We have found that the half-life of a vision is six weeks. Every six weeks people forget half of what their managers have told them about their organization's future, along with the strategies and plans for getting there. People very rapidly fill the void created by this forgetfulness with their own interpretation of where the organization needs to go. The pull back to incandescence can be overwhelming.

You can think of CI as a balloon with a hole in it. Managers need to be constantly blowing into it if the CI balloon is to remain inflated. Given the half-life of a vision, those managers who annually come out of their corner offices to deliver the "Sermon on the Mount" may as well stay in their offices for all the good they are doing.

LEVEL 5. Maintaining level 4 status requires an ongoing and significant expenditure of management's energy. In other words, level 4 status is not self-sustaining So what would make level 4 self-sustaining? The answer is building a critical mass of people who deeply believe in the organization's desired future. Just like a nuclear chain reaction, you want to reach a point where members of the organization, not just management, are talking about the vision and building understanding and excitement for it among their colleagues. When this happens, staff are constantly re-energizing and igniting each other around a common future. When this happens, new staff are rapidly enrolled in common cause by their fellow workers. Common cause has become part of the fabric of the organization. This defines a level 5 CI organization.

What does a level 5 organization look like? If you were a fly on the wall in the offices of a level 5 CI organization, what would you see? Well, you would see people everywhere talking about the difference their organization is going to make in the world. You would see people sharing and building upon each other's ideas. You would see people pushing each other towards best. You would see people with courage who are taking themselves and their piece of the organization to new places. You would see boundless energy for change that moves the organization forward. You would see people so deeply involved and committed to what they are doing that no one has an up-to-date resume. People in a level 5 organization are not even aware of what job opportunities are available with other companies. You would see people caring about the success of the whole as much as or more than they care about their own individual success. You would see an organization that is at least three times more productive than the industry norm.

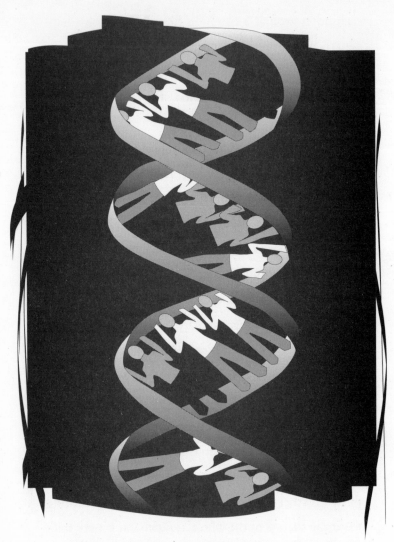

The intertwining of work and life missions is akin to the double helix of life, DNA; this intertwining gives the organization its life force.

CONDITIONS FOR LEADING:
INTERTWINING LIFE AND WORK MISSIONS

Building a high CI laser organization starts with senior management. You can't build cause in others unless you first have it in yourself. You can't touch someone else's heart unless your heart has first been touched. Building cause in yourself starts with first understanding your life's mission: why were you put on this planet? What brings you joy? The answers to these questions point to your life's mission.

It is the intertwining of one's life mission with the organization's desired future that creates cause and energizes one towards great accomplishments. The intertwining of work and life missions is akin to the double helix of life, DNA; this intertwining gives the organization its life force. It is what gives leaders the ability to enroll others in the achievement of their organization's desired future.

Your life's mission is your calling. It is the connection between what brings you joy and the contribution you want to make to society. Aligning one's work with one's life mission is what creates cause. Cause, simply put, is getting excited, being joyful about the positive contribution your work is going to make to the lives of others. For your life's mission to be an energy source you must make it explicit.

You start to understand your life's mission by thinking about it, talking about it and writing it down.

Finding and understanding your life's mission is very much like walking in a fog. You start off in the fog but with each step forward, the fog parts a little and the path becomes a bit clearer. Understanding your life's mission is an ongoing, never-ending activity. Each time you think about your life's mission, it becomes a little clearer to you.

The deeper the understanding you have of your life's mission (your calling), the easier it is for you to align your work life with it. Once you have achieved this alignment, the people around you will feel the passion you have for your work. As a leader, it is only when you have aligned your life's mission with your work that you will be able to lead and build cause in others.

THE BOTTOM LINE

Corporate intelligence is all about building a laser organization and that means getting the organization's energy aligned around common goals. What drives this alignment is nonstop talk about the organization's desired future, the strategies and plans for getting there and why this is worthy of people's time and energy.

Michael Michalko, in *Thinkertoys*, his book on creative thinking, captured the power of corporate intelligence when he said:

> "Imagine your business as a gigantic boat powered by a group of people with their own outboard motors. Without direction, agreement, collaboration, and communication, each person will likely be pointing his or her motor in a different direction, and the boat will founder or turn in circles. On the other hand, if the group comes to a common understanding and agreement about their destination and direction, the members can align their individual motors toward a common goal."[4]

---

4 Michael Michalko, *Thinkertoys: A Handbook of Business Creativity* (Berkeley, CA: Ten Speed Press, 1991).

CHAPTER FIVE

BUILDING EI, RI AND CI
THE LEADER'S RAISON D'ÊTRE

If EI, RI AND CI ARE THE ROUTE to high performance, how exactly do you go about building these three intelligences into your organization, your project or your team? What are the specific activities, events, processes and structures that a leader needs to put in place, undertake and make happen to bring the power of these intelligences to bear? Is instilling these three intelligences into your organization complex and difficult? Does it require years of study and a bevy of consultants? Do you have to invest buckets of money to make it happen?

The good news is that the answer is "none of the above." Getting these three intelligences into your

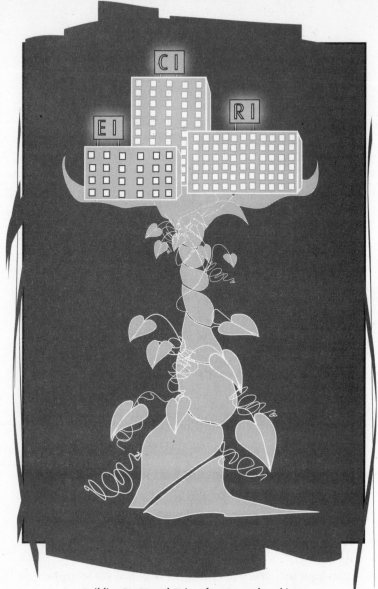

Building EI, RI and CI is a forever undertaking.
Building a high-performance culture starts with leaders
seeing this as their raison d'être.

organization is not rocket science. It is a surprisingly simple process. But simple does not mean easy. It is not easy because it requires leaders to fundamentally change what they focus on, what they put their time and energy into, and how they relate to and interact with their people. Building EI, RI and CI is not an event. It is not something you do and then declare victory. Building EI, RI and CI is a forever undertaking. Building a high-performance culture starts with leaders seeing this as their raison d'être.

To demonstrate the building of the three intelligences, let us return to the case study mentioned in Chapter 4, which we will hereafter refer to as Project Genesis. The organization in this case study needed to replace one of its mission-critical legacy IT systems. This project was large and complex and involved approximately 100 business analysts, systems analysts, programmers, testers and support staff. The management team responsible for running the project was made up of a project manager and eight team leaders. About one-third of the team came from the client organization and the remaining two-thirds came from a large international systems integrator (an external vendor that manages large IT projects).

As mentioned in Chapter 4, projects of this size fail more often than they succeed. The IT industry recognizes this and, whenever possible, attempts to break up large projects into a series of smaller ones. In this case, however, the small-step approach was not possible. The nature of the legacy system being replaced dictated that the approach would have to be all or nothing.

The systems integrator understood the risk inherent in a project of this size and staffed it with some of their most experienced people. Their project manager was a seasoned veteran who understood conventional project management and ruled with an iron fist. He scrutinized everything; no detail was too small for him to pay attention to. This man burned the candle at both ends for project success. The team followed his lead. They worked long hours, heads down, knowing that if they missed a deadline they would be called on the carpet.

The result was a culture that was the antithesis of what we have been talking about in the previous four chapters. People were made to feel bad about their own performance. People were not connected or committed to their colleagues' success. People were committed only to what they were personally responsible for and felt little connection to the success of the project as a whole.

Fast forward 18 months. Based on the rigorous management approach undertaken by the systems integrator, you would think that progress would almost be guaranteed. But after 18 months, there were no tangible results other than mounds of paper. To make matters worse, the systems integrator gave notice that costs were going to increase substantially without any guarantee that the future would not bring further cost increases.

At this point, the client organization bit the bullet and exited the systems integrator. The client organization's assessment of the situation, once the systems integrator had left, was that virtually nothing was salvageable and that Project Genesis would have to be restarted from scratch. If that wasn't bad enough, the one-third of the project team who were client staff felt like failures and wanted off the project. So, the situation was not simply that the project was going back to square one. With the client staff wanting nothing more to do with the project, it was more the case that the project was starting over in a deep hole looking up for some sign of daylight.

But this was a mission-critical system and the client had no choice — they had to start over. Fast forward another 18 months. The system has been fully

After 18 months, there were no tangible results other than mounds of paper. To make matters worse, the systems integrator gave notice that costs were going to increase substantially.

delivered. Moreover, it was delivered at one-third of the cost of industry norm for a project of this size and the error rate in the first three months of production was one-tenth of industry norm. In 18 months, Project Genesis went from worst-in-class to best-in-class. How did this happen?

Well, when the client organization brought in a new systems integrator to restart the project, they did something else that was a little unusual. They brought onboard a project coach. The client was astute enough to realize that the failure of the previous effort was not due to the quality of the people, but rather had something to do with the culture of the team. The client wasn't sure what a winning culture looked like, but they were sure that if they didn't invest in building the right culture out of the starting gate, then history was likely to repeat itself.

To this end, the project coach's mandate was to help the project's new management team build a high-performance culture. I, Ron Wiens, was that project coach. The rest of this chapter delineates what was done to help the project's new management team build the culture that took the project to success.

The premise of this book is that EI, RI and CI

form the core of an organization's culture. The degree to which people believe in themselves, believe in each other and believe in their organization shapes culture, which drives performance. This premise was the starting point for rebuilding Project Genesis's culture.

Now, the three intelligences are not independent. For example, doing something to grow team members' self-esteem (EI) will often grow the level of trust (RI) that exists in the organization. Having said that, we used these intelligences as three separate and independent lenses to see and understand the project's current reality and then to design a program for the transformation of Project Genesis's culture.

BUILDING PROJECT GENESIS'S EI

Project Genesis was restarted. The situation was this: two-thirds of the project team were new, coming from the organization that took over from the previous systems integrator. One-third of the project team, those coming from the client, were simply transferred from the failed project and they came with a lot of negative baggage. The client staff saw themselves as failures. They had lost belief in themselves, belief in their colleagues and belief in the project.

So, the starting point for the cultural transformation program was helping client staff rebuild belief in themselves and their ability to deliver; that is, growing their emotional intelligence (EI). To help achieve this, the project was replanned. And, it was replanned in such a way as to ensure that the first couple of deliverables would be relatively easy to accomplish. We wanted a plan that gave the project team, both its new and returning members, an early taste of success.

It worked! A few weeks into the project schedule, the team delivered as per plan. Admittedly, it was a relatively minor deliverable; nevertheless, it was still a deliverable and provided the opportunity for celebration. This early success accomplished two things. First, it started rebuilding the client staff's belief in themselves. And second, it started to bring the whole team together and make them one.

Managers need to model the behaviors they want to see. When managers visibly demonstrate belief in self and their ability to deliver, they make it easier for staff to grow a similar set of beliefs. Unfortunately, managers will often play it safe when it comes to sharing project plans by not providing any more information than they have to, or by keeping plans under wraps for as long as possible – the theory being, presumably, that this provides maximum opportunity for managers to rejig the plan before going public and being held accountable.

The management tactic of keeping the strategy and plans close to the chest accounts for a lot of jadedness in organizations. If my manager does not believe enough in the plan to stick his or her head over the parapet, then why should I believe? So, we decided to tackle this issue head-on by putting the project plan on a six-by-nine-foot poster, in neon colors, and placing it in the client organization's lobby. By doing this, the project's management team was essentially putting their reputation on the line. This early and public display of the project plan and all of its milestones sent the message to the project team that management was serious and believed in the team's ability to deliver.

The display of the project plan in the client's lobby provided the opportunity for public celebration. Every time a milestone was met, a golden sticker was placed over the milestone. Project staff walked by this public display several times a day and each time they did so, they were reminded of the project plan and their successes to date. There were several other interesting bonuses from this public display. The rest of the client's organization started interacting with the project team, showing an interest in what they were doing and reminding them of upcoming deliverables. The team was never allowed to forget their commitments and they were never allowed to forget management's belief in them.

When doing a turnaround, one of the first things we advise a client is that they allocate half a percent of the project's total budget to celebration. So, if you have a ten million dollar project, this means that you should be allocating fifty thousand dollars to celebration. The reaction is always swift and it is always the same: "Are you crazy?!" It seems that for many organizations, celebration is simply not tangible enough to justify any significant funding. This is understandable because few organizations have experienced the significant return on investment that can come from a well-targeted celebration program. Often, however, when we are called in to effect a turnaround, the situation is so desperate that the client is open to trying something new. This was the case for Project Genesis and as a result the client was open to investing in celebration.

A principle we use to guide our celebration

approach is to celebrate teams in public and individuals in private. The reason is that we want to use celebration not only to build individual self-esteem but also to connect people. By celebrating individuals in public, you run the risk of turning celebration into a competitive process. So, every six weeks, the entire team came together in a town hall (the reason for the six-week period is explained in the CI section that follows later in this chapter). As part of this gathering, teams that had completed a major milestone would be celebrated. The members of these teams would receive a ribbon with their milestone printed on it. By the end of the project, people's cubicles became awash in ribbons.

The system being built consisted of a number of releases spread over 18 months. The first release occurred after six months. This first release gave the opportunity to celebrate the project as a whole and to celebrate the team's collective contribution. You need to appreciate that the client organization had quite a formal culture – suit and tie, heels and hose – and that the project team was housed within the client's premises. The members of Project Genesis were relatively young compared to the client organization. So, we saw an opportunity to use celebration not only to build people's belief in themselves but also to build an identity that connected people to the project.

To celebrate the first collective team success, we presented every team member with a t-shirt. These were no ordinary t-shirts; they were very comfortable, high-quality cotton t-shirts in a variety of colors. On the front we printed the project's logo and on the back we printed the phrase "We Deliver." We then changed the dress code for the project to one that was considerably less formal than that of the organization in which we were housed. The result was that people started to wear their t-shirts to work. On the project floor, you would see a sea of different colored t-shirts, some walking towards you with the project logo visible and others walking away from you displaying the phrase "We

Deliver." Every day, these t-shirts reminded people of their individual and collective successes. The t-shirts reminded people of their ability to deliver and reinforced their belief in themselves. Team members, when they wore their t-shirts, walked differently. They walked with pride. They walked with a strut that said "I can do this." The t-shirts visibly connected people and helped build, across the team, a commitment to the success of the project as a whole.

To help people see themselves as successful, we used "letters from above." These were written on the client's letterhead, individually addressed to the 100-plus members of the team and personally signed by the client's CIO, who was the head of Project Genesis's steering committee. We advised the executive on the writing of the letters. Here's an excerpt from one of the letters:

> "...Your skill, your effort, your professional dedication has literally caused the Phoenix to rise from the ashes. I have been impressed not only with the amount and consistency of your delivery, but also what your client is saying about the work. The feedback on your work has been nothing short of outstanding..."

And what did people do with these letters? They saved them. People don't throw out letters like this; they put them in a drawer and every now and then when they come across them, they reread them and are energized all over again.

To celebrate individual success, we initiated a Project Star Award. This was awarded by one team member to another for individual performance. Here is how it worked. Anytime a team member saw a colleague doing something that contributed to another team member's success, they could at their own discretion issue the award. To do this, the issuer would complete the certificate shown above, entering both the receiver's name and the deed that the individual was being recognized for.

This peer-to-peer celebration of individual success contributed to the building of the recipients' self-esteem and belief in the value of their work. The peer-to-peer program also strengthened the connection between the award giver and the award receiver. This certificate was accompanied by a fuzzy-head doll that became the project's mascot. As people accumulated these mascots, once again, they pinned them on their cubicle walls. This reinforced one of the project's values, namely that success comes from helping others be successful.

To help the team members connect with their success and see themselves as successful, we arranged for articles on the project's accomplishments to be published in both the client organization's newsletter and local industry publications. We then distributed these publications to the team members. What we were doing was using third-party affirmation to help the team members see and appreciate their successes.

In the words of Lou Tice of the Pacific Institute, "You move towards, become, that which you hold uppermost in your mind."

At one of the team's regular town hall meetings, we put the team members in pairs and had them answer the following questions:

"Project Genesis is already a legendary project. It has become a model for other projects within the organization. It is being talked about right across the city. To quote the CIO, 'the Phoenix has risen from the ashes.' But what is really important is how we, the project's delivery team, feel about the project. In the future, when explaining the project to a friend, what is going to stick in your mind? What is it about the project that will cause you to reflect with pride?"

Here's a sampling of the responses we received:

+ "No 'I' in the word Team"
+ "Open, relaxed atmosphere even under pressure"
+ "I've never had so much fun working"
+ "Raised the bar"
+ "So little time, so much work, but we are doing it"
+ "The will to succeed"
+ "Everyone has a voice"
+ "Management has listened and acted"
+ "One team approach"

Building EI requires leaders to look for ways that will help their people hold uppermost in their minds an image of personal and collective success.

We then took each of these responses, had them done up on individual posters and spread them throughout the project area.

We act not according to our potential but rather our belief about ourselves. Whatever image we have inside ourselves of who we are regulates our performance. Leadership is about helping your people grow strong internal images of who they are and what they are capable of.

BUILDING PROJECT GENESIS'S RI

Relationship intelligence (RI) is a measure of how much people care about each other. If we are colleagues, the question is, "Do I care enough about you to contribute to your success? Do I care enough about you to take myself out of my own personal comfort zone and give you the feedback that will push you, the organization, the project, the team, towards success?" Relationship intelligence is a measure of the trust that exists between the members of the team. It's a measure of the team's willingness to come together and speak with the openness and candor that allows ideas to be deeply explored and quickly advanced. In summary, relationship intelligence is what allows people to work together with explosive creativity.

We knew that on the second attempt of Project Genesis we were dealing with a group of people who had previously worked in sub-teams that had been quite insulated from each other. The relationship between the client organization and the previous systems integrator had become quite acrimonious. So, we expected that the client's team members would be cautious in their relationships with the new systems integrator.

We were very much aware that a critical key to the project's success would be the team knowing each other as human beings. Trust is a measure of the attachment between individuals. Attachment is what causes people to care about each other's success. Knowing this, we designed an attachment program to foster connection between team members. This program was also designed to give team members the opportunity to practice open and frank communication.

At our project town hall meetings, we always started with an attachment exercise of some sort. Now, you must remember that we were dealing with a collection of analysts and programmers; many of them had a more meaningful relationship with their laptop than they did with their fellow team members. You can understand why, at least initially, there was little enthusiasm for the attachment exercises, but we did not let this deter us.

What did these attachment exercises look like? Well, at one town hall – and remember, with 100 people present we were in a room the size of a ballroom – I said, "the floor represents a map of the world." Standing in the center of the room, I declared that the spot I was standing on represented the location of the city that we were in. I then pointed in four directions and said that these directions marked north, south, east and west. I then instructed the team members to go and stand on that part of the world that they wanted to visit and explore.

In short order, we had three or four people in one spot in the room holding up their hands and saying, "we're Greece." In another part of the room, another group was exclaiming, "we're the Galapagos," and so on. What this exercise did was bring people together who didn't really know each other. It gave them something in common, something they could dialogue on, something that would facilitate the development of a relationship. Every six weeks, we ran a different exercise to help build people's connections.

As well, in our project town halls, we put the team members into groups of eight and gave them a question that allowed them to explore and assess some aspect of the project's performance. For example, at one session, we asked the groups to reflect on what the project needed to start doing, stop doing and keep doing in order to be successful. We would bring in the project's steering committee and with the project manager present, each team would get two minutes to share their thoughts and suggestions. What we were doing here was giving the team practice in open, frank dialogue.

When a coach is teaching a young child how to skate, the coach has to help the child become comfortable with a new way of moving. The back and forth sliding motion required for skating initially does not feel natural to the young child. It is not a motion that they are used to or comfortable with. So what does the coach do? The coach will take hold of the child's feet and physically slide them back and forth. The hands-on approach helps the child develop muscle memory for the new way. This is a first step in allowing something that was initially uncomfortable to become second nature.

The purpose of the town hall exercises was to build the "muscle memory" that would help the team become comfortable with a new way of working, a new way of being. In essence, we were using these exercises

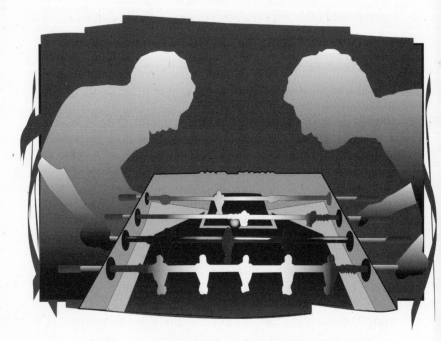

In addition to allowing people who did not know each other to engage in a fun activity, the foosball provided a good physical break from the project's cerebral work.

to assist in the building of a new project culture.

Building RI is going to feel, at least initially, distinctly uncomfortable. Building relationship intelligence is a highly creative process. Building RI requires courageous leadership, because the leaders will be doing things and asking their people to do things that will feel a whole lot different from anything they have done in the past. So the question is, who is going to help move the leader's feet, who is going to help build the leader's muscle memory? The answer: leaders have to build their own muscle memory. Leaders have to have the courage to take themselves to new places. This is the price of leadership.

To help people come together, we organized team breakfasts with the project manager and team leaders doing the serving. We organized potluck luncheons with team members bringing in their favorite dishes. We organized social events such as bowling nights. We purchased a foosball game and placed it in the project's main boardroom. In addition to allowing people who did not know each other to engage in a fun activity, the foosball provided a good physical break from the project's cerebral work.

To build one team and foster productive and

Trust is the organization's lubricant. And for trust to exist, people need to know each other as human beings.

trusting relationships across the vendor-client boundary, we built mixed teams, teams whose members came from both the client and the new systems integrator. As well, we co-located as many people as possible on the same floor, putting teams that needed to work together in as close proximity as possible.

You want to maximize relationship intelligence because you want people to leverage each other's knowledge and abilities. You want to maximize RI because you want an environment in which people trust each other. When trust exists, business happens quickly. Trust is the organization's lubricant. And for trust to exist, people need to know each other as human beings. The leader's role is to help the members of the team connect and develop a personal appreciation for each other. This requires the leader to think nonstop about events and activities that will allow this to happen.

BUILDING PROJECT GENESIS'S CI

Corporate intelligence (CI) is a measure of how deeply the people are connected to what the organization, the project and the team are trying to achieve. CI is all about connecting people to cause; that is, helping people understand how their work makes a difference.

A team with high CI is a team made up of individuals who have a shared vision about what they are creating and building together. When CI is high, people believe in their organization and they have *meaning of work* in their lives. When people are deeply connected to cause there is genuine caring about the success of the whole. This caring is the source of power that delivers extraordinary results.

Cause keeps an organization focused while providing incentive to change. Without common cause, an organization is like one of those silver balls in a pinball game, bouncing around hoping to score well. Without cause, this year ends up looking a whole lot like last year.

To grow Project Genesis's CI, we needed a program that not only made the project's cause explicit for every member of the team, but also kept it uppermost in everyone's mind. We needed a program that would help people see the positive contribution that their work was making to other people's lives.

The prime challenge in building CI is the six-week half-life of a communication, which we talked about in Chapter 4. Every six weeks people forget half of what their managers have told them about their organization's future and the strategies and plans for getting there. As we said in Chapter 4, you can think of CI as a balloon with a hole in it. Managers need to be constantly blowing into it if the CI balloon is to remain inflated.

In Project Genesis, as a result of our understanding of the communication half-life, we held a town hall meeting with the entire team every six weeks. We have already explained how we used the town hall to build RI. We also used this meeting to build CI. At every town hall, we reviewed with the team the project's objectives, plans and progress to date. At every town hall, the client was invited to speak about the future and the role that the business system being built would play in it.

We coached the client to speak from the heart. We also coached the client to write from the heart. On one occasion after a major milestone was successfully delivered, we asked the client to write a letter to the team to thank them for what they had done. We also asked the client to use this letter to help the team appreciate the contribution that they and their work were making to the client organization's future. Once again, this was a letter that was personally addressed to every member of the team and personally signed by the head of the client organization. Here's an excerpt:

"I want to take this opportunity to make you aware of just how much you are contributing to our organization and how much we appreciate that contribution.

Our very future revolves around the system you are building. In fact, to say we are desperate for a flexible system that will support our changing product environment is not an overstatement. Our future, the entire viability of the organization, depends heavily on getting such a system. I am very aware of just how much energy you and your colleagues are putting into this project. We have asked a great deal of you, and you have given even more. Thank you does not seem a large enough phrase for what you are doing for us."

The letter moved people. The letter touched the team's heart and helped them appreciate the importance of their work. The client's letter was received at the halfway point of the project and provided a significant energy boost to the team for the final stretch. Another benefit of the letter was that it was a clear demonstration by a senior executive of speaking from the heart, of speaking with candor. This way of being, this way of speaking, became ingrained in the team's culture. Because of the importance that people attached to their work, they were able to speak hard truths in a caring manner. The net result was that things happened fast, things were not left in the corner to fester.

To connect the entire team to all aspects of the project, we built a command center in the project's main boardroom. In this command center, we displayed along one wall the complete project plan. The plan was color coded with each sub-team having its own color. The plan made visible, for all to see, each sub-team's deliverables and milestones for the coming 12 months. When a team leader was presenting a team's status and introducing any changes to the sub-team's plan, the required practice was for the team leader to use the project wall to make clear the impact of the requested changes on the rest of the project. The various sub-teams would also hold their own team meetings in the command center. All of this was done to help the sub-teams appreciate what they were part of and to help them understand that success was not just about the success of their piece but rather about the success of the whole.

When a team leader went from caring just about

his or her sub-team's success to caring about the success of the whole, there was an accompanying change in how he or she managed. When delivering a status update, team leaders that cared primarily about the success of their own sub-team would talk about the issues that occurred since their last presentation and how they were going to address those issues. Once a team leader embraced the success of the project as a whole, his or her status reports started identifying potential issues and their potential impact on both their own and their colleagues' delivery plans. Team leaders who had embraced the whole became much more willing to ask for help in mitigating a problem before it had a chance to impact the project. The leaders' transition from caring just about their own success to also caring about the success of the project as a whole moved their management style from one of managing the past to one of managing the future.

Just like EI and RI, building CI is a highly creative nonstop process. We did countless things to help the team keep the project's objectives uppermost in their minds. For example, the team was housed in a facility that had particularly high ceilings. So, we used this feature to our advantage. We had small floating blimps made up with the project's objectives and values printed on their sides. These balloons just floated along overhead, and when team members looked up, they would be reminded what the project was all about. We had a plaque made up for every team member's desk that said:

**What information do I have
that would be useful to someone else?
Helping others be successful = project success.**

When staff want to understand what is going on, they usually turn to their immediate supervisors. For Project Genesis, these supervisors were the team leaders. It is important for the project leader to stand up and talk about where the project is going, what the project's objectives are and why achieving them is worthy of his or her time. But if the team leaders are not also standing up on a regular basis and talking about the project's objectives and why achieving them is worthwhile, then the project leader's message will end up falling on stony ground. So, for Project Genesis, we put in place a program to give the team leaders the skills, materials and coaching that would enable them to have deep, meaningful and CI building conversations with their staff.

It is important for the project leader to stand up and talk about where the project is going, what the project's objectives are and why achieving them is worthy of his or her time.

As stated, building CI is a lot like blowing up a balloon with a hole in it. Building CI means working relentlessly at reminding people where you are going and why getting there is important. Building CI requires the entire management team to be working together as one. As Jeanie Duck points out in her book *The Change Monster*, it is not lack of commitment but rather lack of alignment among leaders that is a blocker to success. The laser organization that we discussed in Chapter 4 and all the magical productivity that comes with it starts with a management team that is laser like in its alignment with what it is trying to achieve.

MEASURING EI, RI AND CI

Measurement is a powerful tool in helping you stay focused. Measurements operationalize the principle that "you move towards, become, that which you hold uppermost in your mind."[5] So, to bring the power of measurement into play, we designed a survey that we referred to as the Project Spirit Survey to assess the project's EI/RI/CI. It was a simple survey consisting of 31 questions and we ran it every six weeks as part of the town hall. A sampling of the questions is provided

---

5 Lou Tice, Pacific Institute.

Project Spirit Survey

Sample Questions	Strongly Disagree	Disagree	Mildly Disagree	Neutral	Mildly Agree	Agree	Strongly Agree
I understand how my part fits into the overall project			X				
Our change mechanism is working						X	
We continuously monitor our progress							X
We communicate with each other					X		
I feel free to speak frankly							X
I am proud to work on this team							X
I have fun working on this team				X			

above. Within 48 hours of it being completed, the survey was analyzed and the results simultaneously distributed to all the project's management and staff. At the next project management meeting, the survey results would be reviewed, with one or two actions identified for moving the survey results forward. Once again, the action items would be immediately shared with staff.

The regular running of the survey helped to keep the building of EI, RI and CI uppermost in the minds of the management team. But the regular survey also had another benefit. It allowed us to easily compare changes in survey results over relatively short periods

Sample Questions	1	2	3	4	5	6	7
I understand how my part fits into the overall project				X	O		
Our change mechanism is working				XO			
We continuously monitor our progress				XO			
We communicate with each other			O		X		
I feel free to speak frankly				XO			
I am proud to work on this team				X	O		
I have fun working on this team				X	O		

O Current Survey
X Previous Survey

of time. This comparison turned the survey into an early warning radar, allowing us to see small changes and become curious, ask questions and take action in real time. The radar approach allowed us to deal with mole hills before they became mountains.

SUMMARY

Leaders build self-esteem by helping people connect with their successes. Leaders help their people bond. Leaders grow the trust that leads to open and frank communication. Leaders build common cause, cause that gets their people pulling in the same direction, working for the success of the whole. In short, leaders build EI, RI and CI.

For your typical hard-nosed, no-nonsense manager this represents a lot of soft stuff. But that's the point. In the knowledge worker world, the soft stuff is now the hard stuff. In the more mechanical past, we used to believe that if each part of the organization was successful then the whole would be successful. In the knowledge worker world, the rules for success have changed. If you want a high-performance organization, project or team, it is not good enough to focus just on efficient task execution. Success today means fully engaging the body, mind and soul of every team member. It's the soft stuff that allows you to do this.

We have shared with you, in this chapter, some of the activities and programs that we put in place to build EI, RI and CI in Project Genesis. These activities, as we have said before, are not rocket science. The challenge in building the three intelligences is two-fold. One, it is a nonstop process. Two, for managers and leaders, the building of EI, RI and CI represents a fundamental change in how we go about our day and what we think about.

One final point: We chose to use a large project for our case study. We chose it because as a project it had well-defined boundaries; that is, well-defined objectives and clear and measured outcomes. Project Genesis is a microcosm for the organization as a whole. It has been our experience that the building of EI, RI and CI is entirely scalable upwards to the entire organization or downwards to a single team. The principles and approaches remain unchanged.

CHAPTER SIX

LEADERSHIP IN THE ERA OF THE KNOWLEDGE WORKER

STAYING IN THE LAND OF THE QUICK

IN THE OLD WEST, they used to say that there were just two kinds of people – the quick and the dead. In the era of the knowledge economy the phrase might well be that there are just two types of organizations, the quick and the dying. The knowledge economy has introduced a new set of rules when it comes to managing and leading. The quick recognize this and are embracing new ways of detecting and selecting their leaders. The dying are hanging on for dear life to the ways that brought them success in the past.

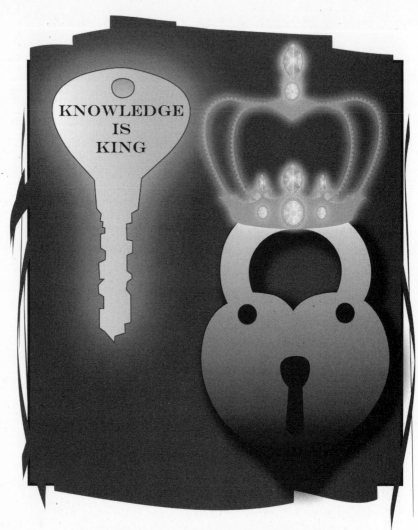

Knowledge is a resource locked in the human mind.

The World Wide Web has taken us into an electronically connected world. Today, people are connected not only to each other but also to each other's knowledge.

We are living in a time in which knowledge is expanding so rapidly that the insight you have at night will be outdated by daybreak. The shelf-life of knowledge will be the same as that of a banana.

Competitive advantage today lies in an organization's ability to exploit this explosion of knowledge. Those organizations that can consistently do this faster than their competitors will thrive and prosper, while the others will wither away.

In today's economy, knowledge is king. Knowledge is a resource locked in the human mind. Creating and sharing knowledge cannot be forced out of people. Every individual possesses unique insights that can be put to use only with his or her active cooperation. Getting that cooperation is key to success in the modern economy. This brings us to a critical driver of economic prosperity, which is having leaders who can engage and leverage knowledge workers. Knowledge workers are quasi-volunteers in that they can choose to make their knowledge known or not and can choose whether they impart all of it, part of it or none of it!

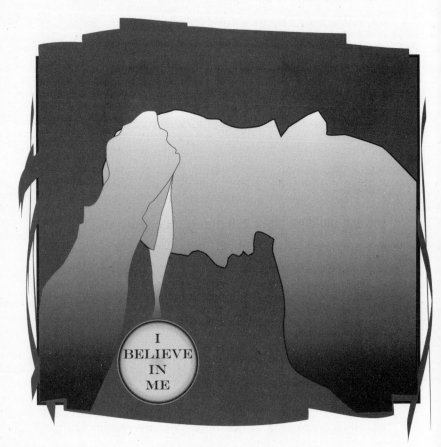

Cultural building block #1 is about helping people believe in themselves.

The job of the leader is to build a culture that gets the knowledge workers working together, freely giving up their knowledge to move their organization towards its desired future. The creation of such a culture requires the leader to focus on three key building blocks:

Cultural building block 1: helping people believe in themselves. People are aware of their strengths and as a result they have the courage to take themselves and their organization out of their comfort zone. This is EI.

Cultural building block 2: building an organization in which people care about each other. This caring drives the trust that allows people to build and create together. It is this caring that allows people to push each other towards best. This is RI.

Cultural building block 3: instilling common cause. People believe that what their organization is trying to accomplish is worthy of their time. It is this belief that fans the flame of accomplishment. This is CI.

In the knowledge economy, organizations need leaders that are capable of building a community of people who

Cultural building block #2 is about building an organization in which people care about each other. This caring drives the trust that allows people to build and create together.

are plugged in, turned on and in tune with their organization. You do this by building within your organization people who believe in themselves, believe in each other and believe in what the organization is trying to achieve. This represents a new way of leading.

Today, however, leadership is in crisis.[6] The boomers are retiring. This represents a mass exodus of leaders across organizations of all types. The downsizing phenomenon of the 1980s and '90s has thinned out development budgets, with the result that organizations have not been making the investment required to replace their departing leaders. The impact of the boomer exodus is compounded by the changing attitudes and expectations of the generations that follow. Unlike the boomers, the younger generations have different priorities with respect to work. They want to be engaged in their work but they want other things out of life as well. This means that fewer are willing to assume the responsibilities and demands of leadership.

So, here's the situation many organizations find themselves in. They are losing leaders en masse.

---

6 Justin Ferrabee, "Leadership Crisis: The Perfect Storm," white paper (Ottawa: Totem Hill, 2008).

They have been asleep at the switch for years in terms of growing the next crop of leaders. All the while, the importance of leadership has been rising. Today's reality is that having leaders who know how to lead and manage in the knowledge economy has become the organization's number one critical success factor.

Can it get any worse? The answer is, yes it can. And what is making things worse? It's the continued reliance on yesterday's criteria for identifying and selecting individuals to manage and lead.

The leaders' mantra can be succinctly summarized as follows:

"It is not my job to deliver.
My job is to build a team that delivers."

Our current recruitment process often conflicts with this mantra. A focus on what the individual has personally delivered as opposed to his or her team's performance can lead to favoring the following leadership types:

- Command and control leaders
- Leaders who are super-technicians
- Leaders with short-term orientations

COMMAND AND CONTROL LEADERS

In today's knowledge economy, a command and control leader will get what he or she asks for and likely little else. Command and control leaders tend to miss out on the additional success their people's knowledge could contribute because that knowledge is never given the opportunity to be released. Command and control leaders turn knowledge workers off, destroy initiative and at worst, cause their team to divest themselves of any sense of personal responsibility for their leader's mission. Command and control leaders turn people into automatons; knowledge workers do not make good automatons.

LEADERS WHO ARE SUPER-TECHNICIANS

Look at any book that lists the attributes of a good leader and you will find a huge shopping list of skills and behaviors. Those responsible for appointments can easily become overwhelmed with criteria to look for. When this happens, recruiters can fall into the trap of simplifying the process by selecting a leader based on the candidate's ability to solve particular problems causing the organization grief at that point in time. In this scenario, a leader is appointed because he or she is technically or professionally smart.

*Quite simply, the workers tune out. The smart leader
has created a ticking time bomb.*

But smart does not always mean smart.

Highly developed technical or professional smartness can actually hinder a leader. People around and below them tend to defer to their leader's smartness. The people they lead stop thinking for themselves. They abandon their own thinking and creativity, and as a result, offload accountability to their leader.

The culture under the "smart" leader starts to deteriorate. Without thinking, without creativity, without accountability, people become disconnected from their work. They become disconnected from outcomes. They show up for work every day and plod along, but the work no longer has any deep meaning for them. Quite simply, the workers tune out. The smart leader has created a ticking time bomb.

Leadership isn't only about being technically or professionally smart. It isn't only about making the right technical decisions. The biggest learning for the too-smart person is that leadership is not about being right, it's about building a creative and effective team that does the right thing. Actually, leadership is about being smart enough to make room for your people's thoughts. Leaders need to create the space for their teams to come up with their own answers. It is this

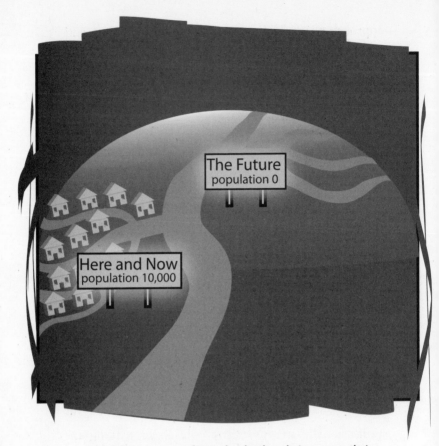

One of the important things that leaders do is prepare their organization, their unit, their team for the future. When the leader lives in the Land of the Here and Now, this preparation does not always get done.

approach that gets knowledge workers engaged and leverages what they know for the good of the organization. For all their smartness, many smart leaders have not realized that their job is no longer to deliver, but to build a team that delivers.

LEADERS WITH SHORT-TERM ORIENTATIONS

There is a natural and understandable tension that exists between a short-term perspective and a long-term one. The organizational problems we face and the rewards we receive tend to reside in the here and now. So there is a natural tendency for leaders to live in the present. However, without a long-term perspective, the urgent will almost always push out the important. One of the important things that leaders do is prepare their organization, their unit, their team for the future. When the leader lives in the Land of the Here and Now, this preparation does not always get done. But one day, the future arrives and the organization, unit or team is not ready for it. The short-term perspective leader has taken his or her organization, unit or team into the Land of the Dying.

The lens that is in use today to identify and recruit leaders was not built to function in today's economy. But we continue to use it.

The good news is that there is a silver lining in all this bleakness. Our organizations are filled with talent. We have the most educated workforce in the history of the human race. And it is the norm, not the exception, that people want to make a contribution. People want their lives to make a difference. So, among all this talent, where are the up-and-coming leaders? Why are we not suffering from an embarrassment of riches when it comes to choosing new leaders? If the potential leaders are there, why are we not seeing them?

Consider the case of the violinist who played in a Washington, DC, Metro station on a cold January morning. He played six Bach pieces for about 45 minutes. During that time, over a thousand people went through the station. Only six people stopped and stayed awhile. About 20 gave him money but continued to walk their normal pace. When he finished playing, no one applauded, nor was there any recognition.

No one knew that this violinist was Joshua Bell, one of the best musicians in the world. He played one of the most intricate pieces ever written, with a violin worth $3.5 million. Two days before, Joshua Bell sold out a theater in Boston where the seats averaged $100.

This is a real story. Joshua Bell playing incognito in the Metro station was organized by the *Washington Post*[7] as part of a social experiment about perception, taste and people's priorities.

So the question is: will talent be recognized in an unexpected context? This experiment says the answer is no! Why? Because context affects the lens we choose to view the world around us. Basically, if we do not expect to see it, we will choose a lens that prevents us from seeing it.

So it is in finding leaders. We are using an outdated lens to search for leaders, so we are blind to the potential that is in our midst. If we want to be one of the quick and not one of the dying, the time has come to change that lens.

So the question becomes this: what lens would help us recognize the individuals in our midst who have the potential to lead and manage in a knowledge economy?

THE NEW LENS

It is not all that difficult to come up with a very long list of criteria that leaders, in the era of the knowledge worker, need to have. The problem with the complete list approach to recruiting is that no candidate is likely

---

7 Gene Weingarten, "Pearls Before Breakfast" (*Washington Post*, April 8, 2007).

to have it all. We end up making compromises and accepting leaders that meet some of the criteria but not others; this is reality. But frankly, some criteria are far more important than others. If we are not careful with the compromises we make, we will not get the leaders we need. So the challenge is to identify that very small set of criteria that are absolutely mandatory for successful leadership in the knowledge economy.

Our experience, gained from working with leaders and organizations around the globe, indicates that there are eight criteria that form the basis for detecting and selecting today's leaders. Furthermore, these eight criteria are arranged into four pairs, with each pair representing two criteria that on the surface appear to be polar opposites. The opposing nature of these pairs goes to the very heart of the challenge of modern leadership.

Each pair represents a behavioral tension. Leaders can eliminate this tension for any given pair by living at one pole and ignoring its opposite. However, this is not a strategy for success. Success in the knowledge economy requires leaders with the ability and skill to flow effortlessly and smoothly between the two opposites as the situation dictates.

The four pairs that define the shape of leadership in the era of the knowledge economy are as follows:

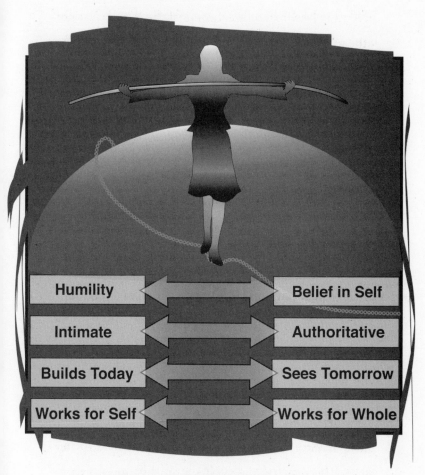

*The opposing nature of these pairs goes to the very heart
of the challenge of modern leadership.*

PAIR 1: HUMILITY AND BELIEF IN SELF

Leaders need the humility that allows them to genuinely listen to the ideas of others. This listening does two things. First, it expands a leader's thought process. Listening gives the leader new ideas and enriched solutions. But frankly, the true impact of genuinely listening is how it transforms relationships. As Stephen Covey says,[8]

> "What happens when you truly listen to another person? The whole relationship is transformed: Someone started listening to me, and they seemed to savor my words. They didn't agree or disagree, they just were listening, and I felt as if they were seeing how I saw the world. And in that process, I found myself listening to myself. I started to feel a worth in myself."

When leaders listen, they build people's belief in themselves. This belief gives people the courage to take their thinking to new places. As W. Chan Kim and Renée Mauborgne point out in their *Harvard Business Review*

---

8 Stephen R. Covey, *The 7 Habits of Highly Effective People* (New York: Simon & Schuster, 2004).

paper "Fair Process," listening does not set out to achieve harmony or to win people's support by accommodating every individual's opinions, needs or interests. Listening is about giving every idea a chance and it is the merit of the idea and not consensus that drives the leader's decision-making. Listening gives people a sense of involvement. If I feel my leader has genuinely listened to and considered my views, even if my ideas are not part of the end solution, I feel that I have contributed. When leaders listen, they build commitment; they build ownership of whatever emerges.

When leaders have the humility to value their people's thoughts and input, something magical happens – there is a sea change in their relationships. Listening takes leaders, for the moment, off their leadership pedestal and places them in a peer-to-peer relationship with their team members. In effect, the humble leader elevates the team and in so doing strengthens the team. A leader that truly listens is showing respect, and showing respect builds trust.

We all want to work in teams that are powerhouses of creativity and problem-solving. But the basis of creativity and problem-solving is creating sufficient intimacy and security for candor to flourish. In high-performing teams, you observe people who are willing to put their preliminary thoughts and rough ideas on the table for all to see. And what do their fellow team members do? They listen, they involve themselves intimately in their colleagues' ideas, they ask enquiring questions, share their own thinking, and as the discussion progresses, they take their colleagues' thoughts and ideas apart. This is the process that helps grow the idea and everyone involved. The end result is a fast-moving team that is pumping out ideas and solutions.

The key to a high-performing team is candor and the key to candor is trust. I need to trust that my fellow team members are interested in my success. It is this trust that gives me the courage to share my thoughts. It is this trust that opens my ears and allows me to hear and take in what my colleagues are telling me. In effect, a listening leader is leading by example and through that example is laying the foundation for a culture of feedback. In this culture, people say what is on their mind, at any time, to anyone, for the good of the whole. As Jim Collins points out in his book *Good to Great*,

"One thing is certain; you absolutely cannot make a series of good decisions without first confronting the brutal facts. In confronting the brutal facts the good-to-great companies left themselves stronger and more resilient."[9]

Listening leads to a culture that regularly puts the "brutal facts" on the table.

When a leader listens, people feel respected and valued. The listening gets people believing in themselves, taking ownership, innovating and going beyond the call of duty. Listening unlocks and leverages the organization's talent. Leaders that have the humility to listen build their organization's emotional, relationship and corporate intelligence (EI/RI/CI). Through listening, the humble leader enables and accelerates change.

On the other side of this polarity is the need for leaders to know when to ignore the distracting thoughts and new ideas that are being constantly whispered in their ear. New ideas are seductive. It is easy to fall in love with the next great idea before you have finished

9 Jim Collins, *Good to Great: Why Some Companies Make the Leap...And Others Don't* (New York: HarperCollins, 2001).

with the previous one. This changing of horses in midstream can become a habit, a habit that will cause an organization to lose its strategic focus.

Many organizations whose leaders proclaim commitment to change often fail to achieve significant results because they have built a culture in which it is the idea itself that is valued and not the implementation effort required to realize the benefits. In such cultures, creativity is considered to be an intellectual proclivity for generating new ideas, new strategies, new policies and new action plans. In these cultures, the idea people are hoisted up on shoulders and paraded around the organization while the implementers are left starving for attention. What the leaders of these cultures fail to appreciate is that the competitive differentiator lies in the Land of Implementation rather than the Land of Ideas.

Ideas are important and choosing the idea in which to invest is critical to an organization's success. However, study after study demonstrates that the really successful organizations are differentiated from the rest by their ability to implement. Once an idea is chosen, the successful leader keeps his or her team focused on investing the time and resources required to transform the idea into their reality.

WHAT DRIVES SUCCESS?

There is a significant amount of research showing that what makes an organization successful and differentiates it from the competition is its ability to stick to it.

- Jim Collins's book *Good to Great* was based on seven years of research involving 1,435 Fortune 500 companies. His research concluded that what moved a company to greatness in terms of its bottom-line performance was picking "one big thing and sticking to it."

- Nitin Nohria, William Joyce and Bruce Roberson, in their paper "What Really Works" (*Harvard Business Review*, July 2003) followed 160 companies over a 10-year period. They concluded that strategy was less important than the ability to implement a strategy and that success came less from the specifics of any given strategy and more from the leader's ability to tightly focus their organization on the delivery of a single strategy.

- Jack Welch, General Electric's former CEO and one of the most successful business leaders of the 20th century in terms of bottom-line performance, was known for picking one major change initiative and focusing his organization on it for three to five years.

An organization can easily generate more ideas than it has the energy to realize. An organization that is unable to choose or attempts to ride multiple ideas under the mistaken assumption that this approach keeps their options open and thereby reduces risk is doomed to paying lip service to the implementation process – there is simply too much to do.

In those cultures in which it is the idea and not the implementation that is valued, the leader will be constantly bombarded with alternate ideas that, if listened to, will distract and pull the organization off its strategic track. What those around the leader are saying often sounds intelligent and reasonable. As a leader, you don't know for certain what the outcome of a given project is going to be and you feel anxious. Leaders are human – and so they are tempted to give way to their fears and the voices recommending distraction. If they do, they abandon the implementation of the existing idea, start the implementation of a new idea, and the cycle of wasted effort repeats itself.

The research carried out by Collins and his team found that those firms that achieved "great" status did not spend any more time on strategic planning than the also-rans. What the great firms did was to stick to

What the great firms did was to stick to it and not allow other seductive opportunities to side-track them.

it and not allow other seductive opportunities to side-track them.

By contrast, those leaders that cannot stick to it create a complexity in their organizations that drives their people away from investing their energy in the implementation process. Strategy is sacrifice; try to do everything and you'll have no plan, no hope, no future.

In the end, when the leader hops from idea to idea, little is accomplished, even though the organization expends a great deal of energy. This is where the leader loses credibility, resulting in people abandoning the leader's strategy and reverting to their own "reliable" agendas. In this situation, the organization starts to resemble the incandescent light bulb, with energy going off in all directions.

Maintaining the strategic focus required for successful change is difficult. But in a culture that does not value the discipline of idea implementation, it is all but impossible. As a leader, you must not let your fears and doubts become the lens through which you view your organization's way forward. As Ralph Waldo Emerson so eloquently said,

> "Whatever course you decide upon, there is always someone to tell you that you are wrong. There are always difficulties arising which tempt you to believe that your critics are right. To map out a course of action and follow it to an end requires courage."

When a leader stays focused on outcomes, the leader is sending a message: "I believe in where I am going." This message builds his or her people's belief in and passion for the targeted outcomes. It builds the organization's corporate intelligence.

Having the humility that enables one to genuinely listen to and be influenced by others, coupled with the inner belief in self that allows one to remain steadfast on the chosen path, ignoring diverting ideas and opinions, is an essential ability for leadership.

PAIR 2: INTIMATE AND AUTHORITATIVE

The question that immediately jumps to mind is, "What place does 'intimacy' have in an organization?" It would not be an exaggeration to say that the answer, for many, if not most, managers is none. This is unfortunate for it demonstrates what is ailing organizations and the teams that make them up – lack of attachment between individuals and their leaders.

What is intimacy in the workplace all about? "Intimate interactions are those that bring us closer to each other through caring about what each person is thinking or feeling. The intent is to enhance connectedness as a desirable goal in its own right."[10] Leaders engage in intimate interactions when they get down off

---

[10] Sonia Nevis, Stephanie Backman and Edwin Nevis, "Connecting Strategic and Intimate Interactions: The Need for Balance," *Gestalt Review 7* (2003):134–146.

their leadership pedestals and get to know their people as people. It also means the leaders opening up and allowing their people to get to know them.

Intimate interactions are not complicated. If fact, they are possibly the simplest of all interactions. They involve leaders showing an interest in people, showing appreciation for their successes, acknowledging their difficulties, and being curious about what is going on in their lives. Intimate interactions are nothing more than two people showing a genuine interest in each other, building attachment and a sense of connectedness. So what is the value of attachment?

Our organizations are filled with talented people who want to do good. The desire to live a life that makes a difference is not the exception, it is the norm. However, we all have our own picture of what doing good looks like. We all have our own personal agendas. We are all working hard but because our efforts are not aligned, collective progress is frustratingly meager. This is why, as we pointed out in Chapter 4, organizations are like the incandescent light bulb: lots of energy is being expended but it's all going in different directions.

In contrast, in those organizations that are moving forward by great leaps and bounds, people have aligned their personal agendas with the leader's agenda. High-performance organizations are laser like in that the people within them all have the same definition of what doing good means. They have common cause. In high-performance organizations, people have chosen to follow their leader into the future.

And what gets people bending their personal agendas to align with their leader's agenda? Well, understanding the leader's agenda for one. Attachment also plays a significant role here. Knowing my leader as a human being allows me to appreciate what he or she stands for. This knowing and appreciation enables me to believe in my leader. And if I believe in my leader then I am much more likely to follow him or her, which means aligning my agenda to theirs. Believing in the man or woman makes it easier for me to believe in his or her dream. This is the power of attachment, the power of intimacy. It builds the corporate intelligence that causes people to bend their personal agendas to the leader's agenda.

Does intimacy have a place in the workplace? Well, if you are interested in building a high-performance organization, the answer is yes. Without intimacy, you may turn around one day to find that no one is following.

There are times when decisions have to be made rapidly. In a crisis, people may have to follow not because they understand and agree but because the leader has directed them to do so. When the system needs to be pulled into rapid alignment, when expediency and speed are called for or when enough discussion has taken place and a decision is required, the leader must be comfortable using his or her authority to provide direction. A leader that does not know when to seize the reins or is not comfortable with using authority is unlikely to have an organization that is living in the Land of the Quick.

Having the ability to get off the leadership pedestal and get close to your people while knowing when to get back on that pedestal to provide authoritative direction or hard feedback or to make a demand is essential for effective leadership. One moment you are a peer, a fellow human being, and the next you're the boss. No one said that leadership is easy!

One final point: there is a connection between intimate and authoritative interactions. "Authoritative interactions are likely to be more effective when there has been a history of intimate interactions."[11] Why? Because when I know you as a fellow human being, I am more likely to trust you. And when I trust you, I am more likely to listen to you and follow you.

PAIR 3: BUILDS TODAY AND SEES TOMORROW

As previously shared, the leader's mantra goes as follows: "It is not my job to deliver. My job is to build a team that delivers."

There are two ways a leader can fail. If the leader's team delivers a poor product or service, clearly this is failure. However, if the team is delivering a terrific product or service but it is the leader who is out in front doing all the pulling, then this is also failure. The second case embodies the "too-smart leader." Everything depends on the leader. Of the two types of failure, the second has the greatest impact over the long term. In the second case, everything is apparently going along swimmingly but when the leader departs, the delivery engine stalls. The leader has not built a team that delivers. The leader, in this case, has left no ongoing legacy; there is little to build upon.

So what goes into building a team that delivers?

---

11 S. Nevis et al., "Connecting Strategic and Intimate Interactions."

Many things, some of which we have already talked about, such as common cause. In particular, the three things that are key to building a team that delivers are:

+ the work processes,
+ the management processes and
+ the culture.

You could argue that this is really two things, with culture being the outcome of the organization's work and management processes since form follows function. This is another way of saying that the organization's processes, procedures and policies are key drivers of the attitudes and behaviors within it, namely its culture. For example, many leaders preach the value of team work and yet their organization's reward systems focus almost exclusively on individual accomplishments. In this situation, the outcome is almost invariably a culture where the focus is "me" rather than "we". Quite simply, asking for behavior "A" while rewarding its counterpart is managing through "sainthood" – expecting people to ignore the messages that the organization's processes and systems are sending them and through divine inspiration to do the right thing. Although management through sainthood is still an approach favored by many, as it avoids the pain of having to change the system – that is, the processes, procedures and policies – its track record is not all that good.

So, if culture is an outcome of your processes, why label it as one of the three things that drive team performance? The reason is that culture is "soft" – generally, it is not something that you can take a picture of. Being soft, it is easily ignored and forgotten. Getting the behaviors and attitudes you want within your organization means treating culture as something that is very tangible. Leaders need to keep their culture goals top of mind so they can deliberately design the processes, policies and procedures to drive the attitudes and behaviors that lead to a team that delivers.

When building their organizations, leaders, even very senior ones, need to get into the weeds without being entangled by them. Leaders need to take meta-responsibility for their organization's or team's processes. Focusing on outcomes is not good enough. Today's knowledge workers are smart, ambitious and hard working. Give them a target outcome and more often than not they, without any intervention from the leader, will deliver.

So, if this is the case, why does the leader need to get involved with process? It is because that while knowledge workers love the challenge and will rise to it, they tend not to think about smoothing the way for the next time a similar piece of work needs to get done. For example, successful delivery is often the result of a series of successful compromises (e.g., budget, timelines and quality levels) and it's the management processes that tend to facilitate these compromises. Management processes, processes that force deadlines and budget constraints, are not usually top of mind for knowledge workers. These processes are a key part of an organization's or team's delivery engine and as such, the leader needs to pay attention to them along with the other processes that drive delivery.

Knowledge workers are interested in the challenge of delivery. They tend to be less interested in building the delivery engine. The job of ensuring that energy is put into building the organization's or team's engine falls to the leader. Without good process, every delivery becomes an adventure, often requiring heroic effort. While heroic effort works in the short term it is not sustainable in the long term. It is the ongoing refinement of process and not heroic effort that builds sustainable competitive advantage.

The leader is the organization's chief architect. The leader must spend time in the bowels of the organization ensuring that the delivery engine is constantly being refined. How things get done is a key component of any business strategy. It is what differentiates organizations. It is where competitive advantage grows.

So, leaders need to be able to operate in the mundane world of process. They need to be excited by building their organization's delivery engine. But here is the rub, and this is where leaders tend to get tangled in the weeds: they need to remember they are having the engine built for others to operate. It is the leader's job to ensure that a delivery engine gets built and built in such a way as to minimize their involvement in its ongoing operation.

Leaders, by keeping the delivery engine on their personal radar screen, are sending the message that they are serious about making their dreams for the future a reality. They are not just idea people; they are implementers as well. This builds their people's belief in their organization and their organization's future.

From time to time, leaders need to be able to pull themselves out of the mechanism that is their organization. They need to let go of the oil can and put the hammer and saw down. They need to move to the sandbox that has "future" written on it. That's right; leaders need to play in the future. And they need to do this regularly.

Future work is very much about whole-brain thinking. You use your left brain to gather the data

*This type of thinking cannot be done by grabbing
30 minutes here and 30 minutes there. This type of thinking
requires blue-sky time.*

– from books, conferences, speaking with people – and you use your right brain to throw all this data up in the air and look for the hidden patterns. These are the patterns that give you insight as to where your world is going and how the rules of the game are likely to change. This type of thinking cannot be done by grabbing 30 minutes here and 30 minutes there. This type of thinking requires blue-sky time. This is two- to four-hour chunks of undisturbed time on a weekly basis.

The challenge for the leader is to have the discipline to set this blue-sky time aside. The future is tomorrow, so it is easy to let the pressures of the here and now rule. But sooner or later, tomorrow shows up and the leaders that have been living exclusively in the here and now end up with an organization that is not ready for tomorrow – an organization that is now one of the dying.

On the other hand, leaders that have little or no time for today and the mundaneness of delivery may think great thoughts but they end up with organizations that are unable to deliver on these thoughts. The 2008 recession saw the demise of a number of great firms whose leaders were noted for their blue-sky capabilities.

Building the delivery engine and figuring out

Leaders need to be able to see and understand the organization's big picture. They need to understand the hurdles and roadblocks that are on the organization's path to success.

where tomorrow is going represent two wildly differ-ent sandboxes. Leaders not only have to be comfortable with and competent in playing in both boxes, they have to be deeply interested and passionate about the unique challenges inherent in these polar opposites.

PAIR 4: WORKS FOR SELF AND WORKS FOR THE WHOLE

Leaders need a competitive streak. They need to be able to stand up and ensure that their piece of the organization gets the funding and resources it needs to be successful. Leaders need to be able to make the case, convincingly, as to why their projects should be given priority over others. They need to be able to mobilize the other parts of the organization to coop-erate and supply what is needed for their team to be success-ful. Successful leaders are single minded. They are like dogs with a bone. They are focused on their team and they are not going to let anything get in the way of their team's success.

On the other hand, leaders need to be able to see and understand the organization's big picture. They need to understand what the organization is trying to achieve. They need to understand how each part of the organization contributes to the achievement of the orga-nization's desired future. They need to understand the hurdles and roadblocks that are on the organization's path to success – not just their own team's roadblocks but also the roadblocks that their colleagues are facing.

Why do leaders need to know about their colleagues' problems? If the leader is focused on the success of his or her own team, how does understanding his or her colleagues' issues help with this success? The answer is, the successful leader is focused not only on his or her team's short-term success but also on its long-term success. If the organization as a whole does not have a future then the leader's team does not have a future, no matter how successful it is today.

Did you know that high-performance organizations sub-optimize the pieces to get that performance? Think about it! High-performance organizations make some of the pieces less productive than they could be in order to achieve an overall gain in performance. This makes no sense – or does it?

Consider the following. Mary is the Director of Product Development and George is the Director of Operations. George needs to retool his operation to make it ready for some new and innovative products that are coming out of Mary's group. The future of the organization looks rosy. The new products are really going to outstrip anything the competition has. But there is a problem. George has lost three of his best people. It looks like his retooling is going to be delayed by six months. This delay may result in the organization losing its market advantage, which would be disastrous for the firm.

Mary is aware of George's problem and so she approaches him with an offer. She says:

"George, how about I loan you three of my best people. They understand operations and with their help you will be able to keep your retooling on schedule. Now this is going to cost me. I will not be able to meet all the objectives that the CEO has laid out for me. But if your group succeeds the future of the firm is in the bag." She also adds, "Now George, you don't get to keep these people. I want them back. In six months you are on your own, so start looking now for their replacements."

George laughs a nervous laugh. He is grateful to Mary; she has just saved his bacon – the company's bacon as well, for that matter. But he knows Mary and he knows that she can play rough, so he just put any thought about keeping Mary's gift out of his mind.

So what happened here? Mary, for the good of the whole, reduced the performance of her group in the near term. This is what high performance is about. Mary sacrificed her group's performance to keep her organization in the Land of the Quick. Enlightened self-interest, you say. Yes, but painful nonetheless for Mary's near-term prospects, especially her current-year performance bonus.

Recently, we were engaged by a high-tech firm whose home base was in Eastern Europe. The country is now part of the European Union. The firm recognized that if it was to survive on the EU's more competitive playing field it would have to up its game. In a meeting with the firm's management team, it became apparent that the firm was rigidly stove-piped. Each department, each team for that matter, operated as though all that mattered was its own success. We introduced the concept of working for the good of the whole and described how this may require, at times, one team making a sacrifice so that another team can be successful. When the presentation concluded, the room went silent. Then, finally one junior manager spoke up and said, *"Sounds like communism to me!"*

More than one person has argued that working for

the good of the whole is expecting too much of people. Their point is that it is simply too difficult to build an organization in which the leaders have embraced this approach. Maybe they are right. Maybe this is why truly high-performance organizations are so few and far between. While this behavior may not be the norm, the prize, high performance, makes its pursuit worth the effort.

Realizing this prize requires leaders who are passionate about what their organization is trying to build and passionate about their own personal success. The tension between these two passions fuels the compromises required for success. Once again, the leader is modeling performance for his or her people. What the leader is passionate about is what his or her people become passionate about. In this case, it results in people who believe so deeply in their organization that they work not just for their own success but for the success of the whole.

CONCLUSION

The lens that we are currently using to see and select the future leaders of our organizations has now passed its "sell-by" date. It needs to be replaced with a lens that gives us leaders who know how to lead and manage in a knowledge economy.

The new lens focuses on eight criteria arranged into four polar opposite pairs:

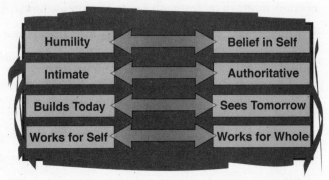

We now need to find leaders with all eight abilities, not just four.

What tends to get rewarded by organizations at the moment is:

+ Belief in self over humility
+ Authority (ability to use rank) over intimacy
+ Seeing tomorrow over building today for senior ranks; building today over seeing tomorrow for junior ranks
+ Working for self over working for the whole

We now need to find leaders with all eight abilities, not just four.

The new lens will help us see leaders who are capable of building a community of people who believe in themselves (EI), believe in each other (RI) and believe in what the organization is trying to achieve (CI). This represents a transformation in how we select leaders and how these "new lens" leaders will lead. But in the era of the knowledge economy, this is the type of leadership that will ensure the organization remains one of the quick.

WHAT DOES IT ALL MEAN?

GETTING TO THE JOY OF WORK

} **So WHEN ALL IS SAID AND DONE,** what is this EI/RI/CI stuff really all about? Well, at the simplest level, it's about delivering a phenomenal lift to an organization's bottom line. But it goes much further. EI, RI and CI encapsulate a model for leading knowledge workers, a leadership model that engages and leverages talent and has the potential to take a society, as a whole, to a higher level of prosperity.

In his book *The Wealth and Poverty of Nations*, David S. Landes presents an economic history of the world and through this lens reveals that the first driver of a society's prosperity is a set of laws that applies equally to everyone within the society; that is, the ruling elite cannot do as they please. Landes suggests that it is this condition that encourages entrepreneurism. When the rules of the game are clear, apply to all and are actually adhered to, people are more willing to invest their time, energy and money into building factories, infrastructure, farms, etc. because they know that the fruits of their labor will not be arbitrarily taken from them.

Landes then goes on to show that the second driver of economic prosperity is the production of knowledge workers. This driver is older than many people realize. In the late 1800s, big German corporations such as BASF, Bayer and Agfa rose and flourished as a result of the competitive advantage provided by Germany's engineering and chemical schools.

> "By World War I, Germany had left the rest of the world far behind in modern chemistry – so far behind, that even the confiscation of German industrial patents during the war did not immediately benefit competitors overseas. The biggest American firms, with the best American chemical engineers, did not know what to do with them or how to make them work."[12]

---

12 David S. Landes, *The Wealth and Power of Nations: Why Are Some So Rich and Some So Poor?* (New York: W.W. Norton, 1999).

For the past 125 years, the importance of knowledge workers to a society's economic performance has been steadily rising. The Western economies have reached the point where their economic prosperity is now directly dependent on their ability to produce large volumes of highly capable knowledge workers – so dependent, in fact, that any nation whose schooling system falters is doomed to a rapid descent down the economic ladder.

So, if the first driver of economic prosperity is the "law of the land" and the second driver is a society's ability to produce highly skilled knowledge workers en masse, then the question becomes, what is the third driver? What will take societies that are already prosperous to their next level of economic performance?

PROSPERITY'S THIRD DRIVER

Today's prosperous economies have the infrastructure, they have the organizations, they have the research laboratories and they have people who are willing to invest in tomorrow. These same economies have filled these laboratories and organizations with the most highly skilled and educated workforce in the history of the human race. Now, the continued prosperity of these already successful economies depends directly on the ability of their knowledge workers to generate new value on an ongoing basis. This points the way to the third driver – leadership, the ability to leverage and align talent. And this is what EI/RI/CI is all about. The three intelligences are the foundation of a leadership model that is targeted squarely at leveraging knowledge workers. EI, RI and CI can raise the performance of a team, an organization or a society depending on the level of leadership that embraces it.

THE REAL VALUE OF EI/RI/CI

So, what is the value of the EI/RI/CI leadership approach? Is it the performance that it drives? Taking organizations and economies to a higher level of performance certainly sounds like a lot. The real and lasting value of the EI/RI/CI leadership approach, however, is not in the economic gains it facilitates but rather in the joy that it brings into the lives of those who work in an EI/RI/CI environment.

ENRICHING PEOPLE'S LIVES

It all comes down to this: If you want maximum performance, you need to build an environment that maximizes people's desire to contribute. The desire to

Success as a leader depends on seeing the job as providing the people you lead with an enriching work experience. And, by the way, as a by-product, you will get phenomenal performance.

contribute is fueled by joy of work. Build people's belief in themselves, connect them with each other, help them see the difference that their work is making in the world and you will get joy of work.

So, here's the leadership paradox: Success as a leader depends on seeing the job as providing the people you lead with an enriching work experience. And, by the way, as a by-product, you will get phenomenal performance.

ABOUT THE AUTHOR

 Ron Wiens, MSc, is the founder of Totem Hill, a company focused on helping leaders build high-performance cultures. Ron has devoted his career to understanding and effecting real, sustainable and positive change in organizations. Over the past three decades, he has been involved in organizational transformation in North America, the United Kingdom, Europe and South Africa. Ron also works with the managers of these organizations personally, taking them through a process of transformation that allows them to build the behaviors and competencies needed for leadership in times of rapid and ongoing change.

Ron is a noted speaker on the topics of leadership, strategic planning and organizational change and is sought by CEOs and other senior executives as a leadership coach. He is the author of many white papers and management publications. His work on organizational transformation has been featured in *CIO Canada* and his white papers on public-private partnerships have been published in the UK's *Local Government Chronicle* and *Outsource* magazines.

Ron can be reached at ronwiens@totemhill.com.

ABOUT TOTEM HILL

Culture is one of the most important – and most challenging – aspects of organizational transformation. It is also often ignored. This is not surprising. An organization's culture is all-encompassing and intensely personal, which makes changing it an especially demanding journey.

Transforming organizational culture demands much more than applying a standard methodology. It demands the attention of the organization's senior people. It demands strategies for change built on insight and compassion. It demands a lot of work and patience.

At Totem Hill, we believe that no organizational transformation can be successful in the long term without successful cultural transformation. From experience, we know that implementing new structures without also aligning the organization's culture will not lead to success. But we also know that with the right approach – an approach tailored to the specific needs of the organization – a culture that is hampering progress can be transformed into a powerful engine for change. At Totem Hill, we help our clients implement cultural changes so that the invisible foundation of their organization supports the achievement of their transformational goals.

For more information, visit totemhill.com.